Healing
the Divorced Heart

Rose Sweet

Healing
the Divorced Heart

devotions
for hope &
encouragement

Advancing the Ministries of the Gospel

AMG *Publishers*

God's Word to you is our highest calling.

Published by AMG Publishers
6815 Shallowford Rd.
Chattanooga, Tennessee 37421

ISBN 0-89957-376-2

First printing—July 2003

Cover designed by Jennifer Ross, AMG Publishers
Interior design and typesetting by Reider Publishing Services,
    West Hollywood, California
Edited and proofread by Mary Ann Jeffreys, Dan Penwell, Warren Baker,
    and Jody El-Assadi

Printed in the United States of America
09 08 07 06 05 04 03 –D– 8 7 6 5 4 3 2 1

To the special messengers God sent me
when I needed them most:
Jim Kidder,
Bradley James,
Steve Porter,
and Howard Lincoln.
You have my love and devotion always.

Contents

CONTENTS

Acknowledgments

These devotions may be short, but writing them takes lots of people who are long on talent. A special thanks to:

Dan Penwell, editor and AMG Publisher's Manager of Product Development and Acquisitions, whose heart is as big as his title.

Mary Ann Jeffreys, Warren Baker, and Jody El-Assadi who, with their red pens, helped perfect the pages.

Florence Littauer whose long-time, loving devotion to me as her friend is a constant encouragement.

All of the CLASS and UpperCLASS (Christian Leaders, Authors, and Speakers Services) staff who offered their prayers and support.

I'm devoted to you all!

Introduction

"Rose, it's Ann. Call me right away."

As soon as I heard the voice mail, I called my friend Ann whom I've known for over thirty-two years. Ann is a nurse and her husband, David, is a pharmacist. From the urgent tone in Ann's voice I wondered if their seventeen-year-old daughter, Katie, had had a minor fender-bender. "What's up, Ann?" I asked.

"David just had a heart attack. He's at Eisenhower in ICU."

I was dumbfounded. David, only forty-nine, had been in good health. Then my eyes filled with tears. "Is he okay?" I asked.

Ann told me he was stable and then described what had happened. After a Chinese dinner the night before, David had felt flushed but dismissed it as probably just the MSG. Later he complained of a headache and then indigestion. In the morning his arm hurt, and while in the shower, he yelled out to Ann that his jaw was killing him. Fortunately Ann had just completed an advanced cardiac life-support class where doctors strongly warned not to let patients be fooled by their symptoms. It might be indigestion, but it might not; pain in the arm and jaw could be tension, but maybe not. Ann's twenty-five years of nursing kicked in, and she quickly and calmly convinced a reluctant David to go to Urgent Care.

David was wheeled in on a gurney and given an EKG. When the doctors came back with the test results and confirmed David was having a heart attack, he bolted upright from the gurney and said, "Now wait *j-u-s-t* a minute!" Even with his pharmaceutical and medical background and even with all the classic symptoms, he didn't want to believe the diagnosis.

They rushed David into surgery where doctors opened and cleared his coronary arteries. The surgeon entered the cardiovascular system through the groin and on the way to the heart, one of David's arteries was apparently nicked filling his belly with blood. When the doctors discovered the abdominal bleeding, they also found that his coronary arteries had collapsed again setting him up for a potential second heart attack. With two major problems to be addressed the doctor decisively told Ann, "We have no choice. We have to take care of the heart first."

Think of divorce as an emotional heart attack. We overlook the symptoms, are shocked to face the truth, and find ourselves dealing with numerous related problems such as where we'll live, who'll get the kids, or how we'll relate to old friends. And just as a heart attack can hit someone who actually invites it or someone who never expected it, divorce strikes the guilty and the innocent, the Christian and the non-Christian, the poor and the rich, those from intact families and those whose families have a history of divorce. But whether you suffer a heart attack or a divorce, you'll have in common the pain, suffering, loss of income, and long difficult recovery period that results.

Divorce can devastate you physically, emotionally, spiritually, and financially. The whole family suffers as members experience their daily routines coming to an abrupt halt. If you're separated or divorced, you may have experienced a "symptom" such as loss of intimacy in your marriage. Or maybe you never saw it coming. You may be one of those people who look back and admit those situations contributed to the problem. Or you may be one of the stubborn few who stay stuck in victim mode. Regardless of how you ended up in the emotional cardiac-care ward, you need expert care, professional support, a practical plan for recovery, and some tender loving care. You'll be dealing with myriad problems related to your divorce, but as the doctor said to my friend Ann, "We have to take care of the heart first."

That's where this devotional book can help. If you'll imagine God as your loving Physician and open yourself up to his healing plan for you, you'll find yourself up and walking again in no time. Within a few months or years you'll be healthier and happier than you ever were before the "attack."

Have you known someone who had a heart attack? It's not uncommon for that person's experience to spur him or her toward making lots of life changes: exercising more, changing eating habits, and developing a whole new approach to physical health. Hopefully, the emotional heart attack of divorce can help you take a look at other areas of your life that can benefit from the deepest healing that only God and his grace can bring.

Not unlike heart medication, this book is filled with daily doses of love and encouragement that can help lead you to wholeness, centered in spirit. How you use it depends on you. You can start at the beginning with Shock and Denial and read your way through to the end, or go right to the areas where you struggle the most on any given day. After reading it once, read it a second or third time.

Consider this book like a prescription medication: Take at least once a day, or as often as needed . . . and call your Physician in the morning!

Shock

What's Happening to Me?

Whoo-oo, whoo-oo, whoo-oo—the siren screams as the ambulance screeches to a halt in front of your home. Loaded down with scary-looking medical equipment, paramedics pour out of the vehicle, rush past the nosy neighbors, and practically bash down your front door. The kids are crying and the older ones are fearfully asking over and over between sobs, "What's happening?" The medical team finds you lying on your bed clammy, weak, and all blood drained from your face. Heart attack? Not quite. You've just been hit by divorce, and you've gone into emotional shock.

Medical encyclopedias tell us cardiogenic shock occurs when the heart is unable to pump enough blood to meet the needs of the body. The symptoms vary from person to person—the pulse and breathing may be rapid or slow, and the skin may be pale or moist. The victim often suffers anxiety, agitation, confusion, and an inability to concentrate. Cardiogenic shock is a medical emergency and, if left untreated, may lead to death. Oxygen is given immediately to reduce the work load of the heart. In many ways your divorce probably sent you into shock and left you gasping for air.

What are some of the symptoms you initially experienced due to your divorce? Are you still sometimes in shock? Do you feel disconnected?

Calling 911 *Dear God, some days I need an extra dose of emotional oxygen—your grace. Help me realize that without it I'll die. Your grace calms me and reduces the stress divorce has put on my heart. Thank you!*

Operator, Get Me Jesus on the Line!

When my husband abandoned our marriage, I went into shock. Although we'd been aware of our problems and had been to see several counselors, I believed we loved each other and were in it for the long haul. I was sure we'd overcome the worst crises and could look forward to many years of wedded bliss. I'll never forget the day he told me he didn't want to be married to me any longer.

My heart raced inside my chest, and my breathing became shallow. I couldn't seem to get enough air to speak while I was trying to convince him to stay. My voice was strained and high-pitched. I felt dizzy. While I was obviously displaying physical signs of shock, he seemed calm by comparison. He left the room, picked up his sunglasses and car keys, walked out, and drove away.

I panicked. I raced from room to room in our home, not knowing where I was going or what I was doing. Was I looking for something? I went outside, came back in, and ended back up in the bedroom where I threw myself face down on the bed to try to calm myself. It was as if my body were moving on its own, desperate to do something to fix the problem. My distracted mind was just along for the ride.

Have you ever felt like that? What did you do?

Talk to the Doctor *Lord, you know that when someone is hurt in my home, and I don't know what to do, I've been trained to move beyond the shock and dial 911. Sometimes I'm still in shock over the divorce and can't think straight. Please help train my mind to immediately call on you whenever I need help.*

Has Your Whole Life Blown Up?

Today while I was writing about the shock of divorce, the U. S. space shuttle Columbia blew into a million pieces. After digesting the horrifying news printed in the morning paper or playing from car radios, most of the nation moved quickly from disbelief into varying degrees of mourning. Special news stories celebrating the lives of the astronauts who died played continuously on television, radio, and the internet. The grieving will continue for most people for weeks or perhaps months, but then the daily details of life will begin to blot out the memory of the painful event.

Not so for the families and loved ones of the astronauts. Some will remain in shock for a long time before they move into mourning. A funny thing about people in shock is that they don't always stare with eyes wide open and mouths open, aghast. They don't always freeze up or appear catatonic as we might expect. People in shock more often seem normal, busily going about their lives. After the news about the space shuttle broke this morning, some people finished their coffee and went back to work, apparently untouched. Are they unfeeling? No, many are simply still stunned and functioning on "autopilot" as a way to deal with the blow. Don't some of us do that after a divorce? We try to avoid the pain we know is coming by keeping ourselves distracted and busy with life: the kids, the house, the job. But if we want to heal, we need to move away from the busyness and face the pain.

Take Your Emotional X ray Have I been functioning on autopilot in areas of my life that need more focused attention? *Show me, Lord, where I need to face the truth.*

Denial

Surveying the Damage

After the space shuttle tragedy citizens from California to Texas reported finding metal fragments in front yards, parking lots, and open fields. No expense was spared in the recovery of the debris and the analysis of what happened. For a while NASA engineers denied that the cause of the disaster could have been a simple piece of foam damaging the wing on launch. They moved beyond denial and now one thing is sure, no space shuttle will go up again before the investigation is completed and the problems are fixed.

Divorce is a lot like the space shuttle explosion. It blows families apart and leaves emotional debris scattered across lives both near and distant. We can learn a lesson from NASA, who sent a crew of highly trained professionals to investigate the cause of the Columbia explosion.

After divorce some people too quickly resume an overscheduled life. Others are so glad to be free of fighting or a miserable life; they don't want to examine the past. Many frantically begin the search for a new partner to ease the loneliness or fill the empty spot in the family structure. Some slam the door on any thought of a future relationship and bury themselves in work or parenting. All are in varying ways giving in to denial. But if they don't take the time to find the mental, emotional, and spiritual weak spots that led to the blowup of their marriages, they're simply inviting another tragedy into their families' futures. What about you? Do you really want to go through all that pain again some day?

Take a Heart Pill *Lord, I don't want to be so foolish as to ignore the problems in my life that need fixing. Will you help me stop denying what part I may have played in my divorce so that I can come to complete healing? It might be a bitter pill, but please show me today what I was denying yesterday.*

Clogged with Emotional Cholesterol

As a child on Sunday mornings I'd sit at the breakfast table and watch Dad salt his scrambled eggs. He always ate bacon and eggs, toast and jam or flaky buttermilk biscuits with honey, lots of hot steaming coffee, and tons of butter. Dad sliced a pat of butter, placed it on the corner of his toast, covered it with a teaspoon of marmalade, and took a bite. He repeated the same steps until the bread was gone . . . along with the whole stick of butter.

My father eventually discovered he had clogged arteries and was a prime candidate for a heart attack. After his quadruple bypass surgery, our whole family had to go to the hospital to watch a video about how to eat healthy to avoid heart problems. But Dad was in denial. He kept eating that butter until he had another bypass . . . and another . . . then a heart valve replacement, and finally an angioplasty. His denial nearly cost him his life and cost all of us lots of anxiety. Others in our family began to watch what Dad ate, warning him and worrying about him, and being drained by the job of being health monitors. When parents don't take care of themselves, children often assume responsibility God did not intend for them to have.

Emotional heart problems are the same, especially after divorce. Take responsibility for your emotional health. Don't deny how badly you or your children have been hurt. But, you say, everyone seems okay. We're feeling better. We have no obvious symptoms. Could you still be in denial about something? Have you positioned your loved ones to take care of you because you aren't taking care of yourself?

Take Your Emotional X ray *Lord, please show me where I may still be stuck in denial. I don't want my heart's arteries to be blocked from receiving the fullness of your healing.*

But My Kids Are Okay!

Despite his parents' constant fighting and eventual divorce, four-year-old Tommy seemed okay. His routine was consistent; he did fine in preschool and loved to race his tricycle around the backyard. His parents made sure he ate well and got enough sleep. As he grew his Mom and Dad faithfully attended his school events, participated in his sports schedule, and took him to the doctor when he was ill. Since everything seemed okay on the surface, Tommy's parents stayed in denial about the effects of the divorce on their son. Friends who'd also suffered divorce advised Tommy's parents to get him to talk about his feelings and fears, but they refused. They were afraid to see the truth. If Tommy seemed okay now, surely there was no reason for future concern.

The consequences of a broken family often don't show up for years, like the arteries of a heart that are slowly being plugged up with plaque. Tommy missed living with his father but learned to stuff his feelings to keep Mom happy. His mother made Tommy, her "little man," feel special for always being there for her. The boy became his mother's emotional caregiver and companion. When he got older, he resented the smothering closeness and began to rebel. Formerly an A student, he began to choose bad friends, took drugs, and got kicked off the sports team for poor grades. Tommy's distraught parents wondered what had happened all of a sudden. They were, and still are, in denial about the long-term effects of their divorce on Tommy. Have you underestimated what effects divorce may have had on your children?

Doctor's Rx Am I in denial about the effects or possible future effects of divorce on my children and me? *Lord, send me wisdom and courage to look squarely at reality.*

Please Don't Make Me Face the Future

Upon hearing Jesus predict his own death Peter, falling into denial, said, "Never, Lord . . . this shall never happen to you!" (Matt. 16:22). Jesus had to jolt Peter out of denial by rebuking him, saying, "Get behind me, Satan! You are a stumbling block to me" (verse 23). I've always felt sympathy for Peter's chastisement, because I know he loved Jesus more than anything in life. Not only had he given up everything to follow the Master, but Peter was the first of the disciples to acknowledge that Jesus was the Messiah. Because of his deep love for the Lord, Peter was afraid for Jesus and what might lie ahead for all of them. It was Peter's fear that brought on his denial.

Fear is always the underlying emotion when denial shows up. Denial is simply the human heart afraid to let go of what it wants. You want to believe your spouse would not do this to you. You want to believe your spouse might have worked harder to make your marriage work. You want to believe in your dreams of a long married life. You want to still be married. You want your children to have a two-parent home. You want a comfortable, uncomplicated life. You want to believe it was entirely his fault. You want to hurry and get through this ordeal and be happy again. Look at all the "wants!" We're all like this; when these wants are threatened by loss and we're afraid to think of the pain we know will come, we stay in denial.

Whether Peter's fear of Jesus' coming death, or our fear of facing a painful future, we all try to hide under denial even when we love God.

Today's Treatment I am going to become more aware of the role fear plays in my life. *Lord, give me the strength to let my faith in you replace any fear that feeds my denial. Thank you for the grace that empowers me to choose faith instead of fear.*

13

Anger

Hot or Cold, It's Still the Same

Maria opened the envelope from her ex-husband's attorney and quickly scanned the official court documents. Her chest tightened when she read that her ex-spouse was not only refusing to pay the children's orthodontist bills but demanding more visitation time with the kids. Maria wanted to scream, gouge his eyes out, and cry at the same time. Have you ever felt like that?

On more than one occasion God got angry at his people's disobedience. If God can experience anger, then it's natural that His creatures feel ire at injustice too. The problem is that we often hang on to our anger, as righteous as it seems, until it grows into bitterness. We might use anger to control others and get our own way. Sometimes our anger fuels other sins like unkindness, gossip, or revenge. That's when anger is a sin that needs to be confessed and forgiven.

Maybe you're hot with anger at your ex-spouse or others. It might be a long, slow boil, seething unforgiveness. Maybe you try to minimize anger by calling it "irritation." Some angry people are cool outside but burning with bitterness inside. Take your emotional temperature by checking your thoughts, breathing, and tone of voice. When you're emotionally hot, it's time to cool the anger. Since anger is rooted in our fear of not getting our way, or fear that the other person will hurt others or us, we can counter our anger and the related fear with faith in God to deal with the person and to care for us.

Take Your Emotional Temperature Sometimes I'm afraid my children or I won't get what we need or want. I don't have to burn with anger because today I choose to believe God's promises that he will take care of us . . . in his way and in his time. Can I wait for that?

I Want! I Want! I Want!

Our mothers told us to handle anger by saying, "Shut up and eat it." Then feminism challenged women to quit being doormats and told them, "Stand firm and mean it." Boy, did they!

The last few decades have seen each generation of women demanding more rights at every turn, often ignoring the rights of others, or the moral and social responsibilities that come with rights. During the same time men were told to get in touch with their feminine sides; women hoped that with the tenderness of feminine energy men would quit being so angry and controlling. What did women get? Sometimes two extremes: Angry, threatened men who told women to shove it, or confused wimpy men who could cry at movies but who didn't quite know what they were supposed to be. If a woman ended up with one of these two extremes, it only made them angrier.

Anger is usually rooted in the fear of not getting what we want. After a divorce we usually have a long list of "I wants," and we think we deserve it all. Have you checked your list of "I wants" lately?

What about what God wants for you? If you truly believe he loves you, wants the best for you, is always there to help you though anything, then why don't you let go of that which you desire and turn your heart to him? Perhaps you lack trust in God. It's usually that simple. Even those who believe in God and love him may still have trouble trusting him.

Take Your Emotional Temperature Am I angry because I don't really trust God will take care of me? *Father, forgive me for not trusting you more.*

Anger Wears Many Masks

Sara complains endlessly to all her friends about her divorce. Mary never talks about her divorce and thinks she's not that affected by it. Jack is so angry with his ex-wife that he yells at his kids, his friends, and even the clerk at the grocery store. Art beats himself up emotionally for all the mistakes he made in his marriage. Inward, outward, or dumped all over everyone else, anger wears many masks. You might recognize yourself as:

The Stuffer: You stifle anger by engaging in activities that numb your feelings. You might stand in front of the refrigerator looking for something to shove in your mouth when you really want to shove someone into oncoming traffic.

The Ambusher: You take your anger out on others, waiting to catch them, set them up, or pull them into your dance of rage. Yelling and screaming are like breathing to you.

The Saint: You pretend you aren't angry, only disappointed. Subtly, shaming words are your way of releasing your anger. You never yell, but you passively punish those around you so you can maintain your holy facade.

The Whiner: You aren't afraid to let others know you're unhappy (angry!), but you do it by incessant complaining, nagging, whining, and grumbling.

Today's Treatment Go buy a book that teaches techniques for handling anger. Read it. Practice on your friends. If you get angry, don't throw the book at anyone!

Loss

A Long List of Losses

Heart disease brings huge losses. After a heart attack almost all the body's systems go out of balance. The patient loses energy and strength; appetite decreases as does weight. Time at work, or even the job itself, might be lost. Financial security, opportunities, and dreams are often lost. What else is lost? Time spent with family and friends, hopes for future health, activities one used to enjoy, foods one used to love to eat. Most people who recover from a heart attack don't stop to take a thorough inventory of things that change and things that are lost. If they did, they might spiral into depression or even despair.

Loss can be a profoundly sad experience for the human heart. Loss implies we had something or hoped to have it, but we no longer possess or hope to possess it. Did you know God purposely created us to both have deep desires and feel profound loss? Most importantly, he did not create us to desire *only* love, marriage, children, jobs, security, justice, peace, and joy; he made us to first desire him.

No matter our circumstances, our joy will return when we remember God can raise us up above all loss and pain. When you're tempted to wallow in self-pity over your losses, imagine if you lost hope of having his love, protection, and provision. How terrible would that loss be?

Even though losses incurred through divorce are heavy on the heart, it's "heart" we should never lose.

Take Your Emotional X ray Have I lost heart? *Lord, help me to remember your infinite love.*

Sometimes in Losing We Win

 Let's face it: the only thing most of us want to lose is weight.

Fat, cellulite, adipose tissue—whatever you want to call it — we are burdened with too much of it in all the wrong places. I recently read "Real Fact No. 106" on the inside of a Diet Snapple Peach Tea lid—YOU WOULD WEIGH LESS ON THE TOP OF A MOUNTAIN THAN AT SEA LEVEL. It may be a worthless piece of information to some, but I think there's a spiritual principle there.

We sometimes refer to "mountaintop experiences" when we are feeling close to God. The more mentally and emotionally connected we become with our Creator, the higher level we can reach spiritually. Those who have continued to reach higher planes in their spiritual journey know that the trip up the mountain always involves some struggle, more than one dark night, and the letting go of fierce desires. Spiritually integrated people have learned to let go of many of their "I wants" and have trusted God to meet their needs in other ways.

Although it's painful, divorce can be a time when we begin to let go of some things to which we have been holding on too tightly: desires for pleasure, demands for happiness, expectations that are unrealistic, selfish desires for revenge, or addictive passions that distract us from our pain. Do you want to be lifted up? Then what do you need to lose?

Daily Dose of God's Word "I will exalt you, O LORD, for you lifted me out of the depths and did not let my enemies gloat over me." (Ps. 30:1)

Thank you Lord for making my heart lighter this day!

What's Bugging You?

 Have you ever seen a field that's been eaten to the ground by locusts?

Fierce armies had nearly wiped out the Israelites. They were devastated by great losses, many of which were direct results of their continued disobedience to God. Since shepherding and farming were the major occupations among the wandering people of Israel, the prophet Joel used familiar word images to exhort them to turn back to God and avoid the "plagues" that would befall them for their sins. He painted word pictures of invading nations that had the fangs of a lioness, nations that ruined fields, dried up crops, and destroyed grains. He described their ongoing sufferings as "the years the locusts had eaten." Jesus also illustrated spiritual principles with his parables about a vineyard, a mustard seed, a coin, and oil lamps.

You might feel gnawed down to the roots by the locusts of divorce: financial loss, emotional loss, physical loss, romantic loss, and sexual loss. Almost every area of your life has been devastated. Even if you're happy to be out of an abusive situation, there's the loss of your hopes and dreams and losses you don't yet know about but which will be felt in the future. But God has a promise for you. The prophet Joel used word pictures that should fill your heart with hope: "Be glad, O people of Zion, rejoice in the LORD your God, for he has given you the autumn rains in righteousness" (Joel 2:23).

God will send whatever "autumn rains" it takes to quench the dry times and bring you a rich and abundant harvest again. Can you just be patient with his timing and his method?

Daily Dose of God's Word "I will repay you for the years the locusts have eaten." (Joel 2:25)

Half Empty . . . or Half Full?

Through divorce I lost my husband, lover, companion, friend, and partner. I lost the only son I'd ever had, my sweet young stepson, Mikey. When the house went into foreclosure, my twenty-year credit history was ruined. I lost speaking engagements, income, and credibility in the marketplace. I had to sell my wedding ring, jewelry, furniture, and my beautiful piano just to pay bills. Thankfully I still had friends who helped me move out of my large home. Sadly, I had to leave a gorgeous kitchen where I frequently entertained and a backyard loaded with fruit trees to a small apartment with crabgrass, a tin-roofed carport, and a kitchen for one.

Living by myself, I ate alone and rarely cooked. Each night I came home to an empty house and an empty bed. I lost the joy of attending school plays, tucking my stepson into bed, and planning family vacations. For the first three years after my divorce it was too painful to buy and decorate a Christmas tree by myself. This page is too short to list the other losses I felt at work, at church, and in the community.

But guess what? I chose to focus on and believe God's promises. I was willing to wade through the grief and be content with what I had in that season of my life. I asked God to change my attitude to one of gratitude for the roof over my head, the work that came in regularly, my friends, and even the little things like . . . cute shoes on sale! I worked through grief to come closer to him, and he made good on his promises to me . . . the same promises he has for you. I am more richly blessed today than I ever was, and you will be too.

Doctor's Rx Read Joel 2:18–27 slowly and thoughtfully, then be quiet and just listen.

Depression

Wash Me Clean, O Lord!

When I went through my divorce, there was a period of almost a week where I didn't even get out of bed. I didn't shower, dress, or even brush my teeth. I smelled bad and looked even worse. I remember about the third day I walked past the mirror in my hallway, stopped, stared at myself, and spat out, "You're P-A-T-H-E-T-I-C!" And I was.

Self-loathing is common when the person we'd really like to hate is not in the house anymore. We don't want to take our anger out on our children or other loved ones, so all that hurt, anger, bitterness, fear, and anxiety turn inward and flow though our veins like poison. If we're emotionally exhausted and have no energy left, anger, hurt, and bitterness can fuel genuine depression.

If you go through days where you hate yourself, imagine someone you love feeling the same way. Like a caring nurse, if you saw someone swallowing all that emotional poison, wouldn't you put your arm around that person and help stop the self-inflicted pain? You can begin to gently lead yourself through depression by taking yourself to the arms of God's love, forgiveness, and grace. Ask him to forgive you for the times you wallowed in self-pity, fear, or anxiety. Are you truly sorry? Then you are truly forgiven. Feel his warmth run over you as he washes you clean and anoints you with the fragrance of his love.

Band-Aid for Your Soul Spend extra time in a nice hot bath or shower, and let your body feel what your soul needs. Lather up, get rid of the emotional poison, and spray something fragrant on afterward. Thank God for small pleasures, and make sure you do it again soon.

Slow Down, You Move Too Fast

According to a scientific report presented to the American Psychosomatic Society meeting in early 2003, depression prompts many people to gain weight. This triggers the release of inflammatory molecules that block coronary arteries and threaten the heart. The chain reaction helps explain why depressed people are 64 percent more likely to suffer a first heart attack than those who are not depressed.

Among patients who currently have heart disease or who have had a heart attack, the depressed in this group are two to four times more likely to have a heart attack. That's pretty depressing news.

Like the medical study, unofficial statistics about divorced people, whether churched or unchurched, point to the likelihood of a repeat event. Those who have already suffered the "heart attack" of one divorce are two to four times more likely to experience divorce again when they remarry. It's important to avoid hasty remarriage; instead, slow down and carefully move through all the healing steps, even if that involves a time of depression. It's actually a good thing we slow down during depression so our hearts, minds—and bodies—can have the time to be repaired and restored.

Divorce is depressing, all right, but less so if you temper the underlying fears with a hearty dose of faith.

Daily Dose of God's Word "Heal me, O LORD, and I will be healed; save me and I will be saved, for you are the one I praise." (Jer. 17:14)

Wake Me When Dinner's Ready

Some people say sleeping too much, gorging on comfort foods, and crying over old movies are signs of depression. Are they kidding? That sounds like a good day to me!

Sometimes depression is staying stuck in some deep, emotional cavern filled with hurt, anger, or hopelessness. Because God created us as chemical beings with minds and bodies that influence each other, depression may require serious counseling and drug therapy to bring us back into balance. At times, however, depression is merely a temporary shutdown enabling us to grieve.

God created us to have heavy hearts and shed tears when we feel loss. Like a cleansing process, grief releases all the emotions that have built up over the loss. There's no shame in grieving even when we do escape into the pantry, the bedroom, or the mall. In our society when someone in the family dies, we usually take off work, shut down the office, go home, and prepare a big meal for everyone to enjoy while we comfort and console one another in our loss. The same goes for divorce. In our grief it's not uncommon to use food and sleep as ways to ease the pain of the losses we feel. The problem occurs when we stay stuck in self-comfort and forget to move through and beyond the grief.

Are you overindulging in some area because of your grief? Perhaps it's time to work through the hurt. Remember that grief *moves on*; depression *hangs on*.

Take Your Emotional X ray Am I hanging on or moving through my grief? *Lord, reveal the truth and then set me free!*

Good Grief

Did you know Jesus sometimes got frustrated?

Scripture tells us several times that Jesus was deeply grieved by the people's continued lack of faith and obedience. For nearly three years he'd been trying to explain in simple terms the good news of salvation and the promise of heaven for everyone who wanted it. But did the people listen? One day Jesus spoke to the crowds that included the hard-hearted Pharisees. He began to warn them, much like a fed-up parent lecturing beloved children. "Woe to you, teachers of the law and Pharisees, you hypocrites!" (Matt. 23:13). He continued with six more "Woe to you's" and then he called them blind guides, fools, snakes, and a brood of vipers. Do you think Jesus was more than a little upset? He was surely as angry and frustrated as we are when the ones we love will not listen to us and refuse to do the right thing.

After this impassioned warning, Jesus cried out, "O Jerusalem, Jerusalem . . . how often I have longed to gather your children together, as a hen gathers her chicks under her wings, but you were not willing" (Matt. 23:37). At that point he must have heaved a huge sigh and let grief flood his soul. He was grieving over the reality of the situation, over not having what he desired for the people. He was frustrated, maybe even depressed.

Have you ever felt like you were beating your head against a wall when someone you love, or used to love, just would not see the light? It's draining. It's depressing. It's grief over the loss of something you desire. Sometimes that's all depression really is.

Doctor's Rx Begin to believe that some types of depression are normal and natural.

Biblical Blues Brothers

When grief overcame him, did Jesus take extra long afternoon naps, eat more sugary dates, or linger in the marketplace, perhaps buying an extra trinket or two? I doubt it, but that's probably what I would have done.

We don't know everything Jesus did to overcome sadness or stress, but we do know that when things got intense or sad, he did one of two things: he went off with his closest friends, or he went off to be alone and pray. Depending on our natural temperament, some of us will want to be alone to process our grief and recharge our batteries. In times of sorrow others seek the solace that only best friends can give.

Mishandling grief by hiding from others or even from ourselves delays healing that needs to take place and can throw us into depression. Some of us in depression would prefer to stay in our caves for forty years, coming out only for food and an occasional walk to the mailbox. Some healing hearts need isolation, but too long away can cause us to turn inward and become perpetually self-focused. That's sinful.

The opposite indulgence is constant interaction and involvement with others so that we don't have to face our pain. Those who can never be alone will always miss out on the sweetness that solitude, especially in the company of a loving Lord, can bring to a hurting heart.

Which is your tendency? Or do you swing back and forth between both?

Talk to the Doctor *Lord, help me quit avoiding reality. Help me come out of my isolation and face the world. And when I stay too busy with others, help me overcome the fear of escaping to be alone with you.*

Guilt

Meet a Six-Time Loser

No one probably felt guiltier about being divorced than the Samaritan woman at the well.

She'd been married five times and was living with a man who was not her husband when she met Jesus under the noonday sun at Jacob's well. Other women in the town went to the well in the cool of the mornings or evenings to gather daily water supplies, but this much-married woman had been socially shunned. Cast out from the circle of mothers and daughters, sisters and aunts, she was forced to go alone in the heat of the day to fill her clay jar.

Jesus was there to give her the gift of his living water, but he had to make sure she was ready to receive it. When she asked for the water that Jesus said would quench her thirst forever, he challenged her, "Go, call your husband and come back" (John 4:16).

Great, she probably thought. *Now I have to bring up the whole sordid truth to this stranger. Should I lie and keep up appearances or tell the truth?* No matter her outward behavior, the woman probably carried more than water on her shoulders. The weight of repeated failure, shame, and guilt was more than she could bear. Maybe Jesus knew she was ready to unload it all when he invited her to be honest with him. Perhaps she sensed that there was no condemnation coming from the Nazarene. "I have no husband," she confessed, and Jesus confirmed that he not only already knew all about her, but still wanted to give her his gift.

Take Your Emotional X ray Have you done or said anything before, during, or after your divorce that causes you guilt or shame? God only wants you to be honest, admit it, and receive his abundant love, grace, and forgiveness—his living water.

Twenty-Four Carat Guilt

After my divorce, my mind continually recycled memories of times I had failed my husband. If only I had been more patient. If only I had focused more on his strengths and not so much on his weaknesses. If only I had been more humble, or kind, or loving. The "if onlys" jammed my thoughts like logs in a stream, blocking me from peace and serenity.

Of course he had his faults, and he was the one who chose not to stay in the marriage and work things out. But God's grace helped me keep my focus off my ex-husband's actions and on my own attitudes. I wrestled with the guilt of my own shortcomings—my own sins—until I called my ex and asked him to forgive me for any ways I had failed as his wife. I couldn't have done it unless I'd already known, despite my weakness, how deeply loved and accepted I was by God. Seeking forgiveness set me free.

False guilt is rooted in fear of being rejected, of not measuring up. Genuine guilt, on the other hand, is a heartfelt conviction from the Holy Spirit—a grieving over what we have done or failed to do. We don't worry so much about how others see us but how we let others down. Genuine guilt allows us to take full responsibility for our actions or attitudes and can position us to seek forgiveness, to reconcile, or to make reparation. It's the beginning of restoring peace in our lives.

Doctor's Rx Do you need to call your ex-spouse, no matter what that person may have done to you, and seek forgiveness for your own attitude or actions in the marriage?

Red Light, Green Light

I love it when my house is clean, my work is caught up, I have cash in my wallet, my car is washed, and the gas tank is full. But if you're like me, you forget to get gas until the gauge is almost on empty. Thankfully the manufacturer put extra warnings in my Toyota Solara. The gauge warns me when my fuel level is going down. If I continue to ignore the gauge, a bright red light comes on giving me one last warning. If I ignore that light, I run the risk of being empty, stranded, and in possible danger.

God created us not only in his image but, I think, in the image of a car! He knows we have to go the distance and keep running right. He's installed a sophisticated system of gauges and warning lights to tell us when something needs attention. If we ignore them, we're in trouble. Our conscience starts to bother us when we've done something wrong. Our stomach may feel queasy when we have something to hide, or we cheat, or steal. We sweat when we tell lies. We can't sleep when we feel guilty. All of these mental, emotional, and spiritual "gauges" are trying to tell us we need to take care of a problem . . . now!

Guilty feelings are warning lights that, if heeded, can bring us back into fellowship with God and those we may have harmed. From that perspective, guilt is a gift. Have you ever thought to thank God for feelings of guilt?

Take Your Emotional X ray Take a look at your dashboard. Is a red light flashing somewhere deep inside? *Lord, please show me where I need to pay attention so that I'm not stranded in sin. Fill my tank with your grace and forgiveness!*

It Doesn't Hurt . . . Really!

God designed warning signs to protect the human heart. Angina is the medical term for tightness or shooting pains in the chest. When a person experiences angina, a heart attack may not have happened yet, but the pain is a signal that should not be ignored. It means arteries are blocked and the heart has to pump harder than it should to get blood flowing to other parts of the body. Heart attack, even death, may be imminent.

When symptoms of a marriage in danger are ignored, the marriage dies and divorce may occur. For years we may have felt, but ignored, guilt about nagging our husbands, ignoring our wives, isolating from our families, or seeking inappropriate pleasure and satisfaction outside marriage. Whatever we did or failed to do, we learned to ignore our guilt. And when it screamed louder and louder, we just turned up the volume of our lives, drowning out the signal God created to keep us safe and healthy.

If you learn anything from divorce, learn that feelings of guilt or regret are there to help us, not make us feel bad. If you feel genuine guilt about anything in the past, quit running from it. Turn around, *face it, embrace it,* and *erase it* through confession and forgiveness. Ignored guilt only blocks our hearts from God's free-flowing grace and from giving and receiving abundant love.

Doctor's Rx *Lord, forgive me for ignoring your signals. Help me not to fear facing my guilt, and to understand that it will block my heart from your grace if I ignore it.*

What You Did, Not Who You Are

Guilt is a legal term ascribing responsibility for wrongdoing. If you're guilty, you pay the penalty. Shame, on the other hand, is a felt emotion that calls for the Master Physician's touch.

In the Old Testament, the psalmist Asaph wrote of his enemies and begged God, "Cover their faces with shame so that men will seek your name, O LORD" (Ps. 83:16). Shame ought to bring us back to God. When a godly person feels ashamed, he'll naturally be reminded that while he is feeling lower than low, there is indeed Someone who is higher than high. True shame is a heart response to our having done something wrong, and if our relationship with God is healthy, we'll repent, and the shame will be gone. And oh, how deeply he loves us and wants to restore us. But as long as we think we are God, we won't seek God.

Sadly, some divorced persons feel unmerited shame, simply because of having divorced. Remember, no matter what we do, or how we behaved in our marriages or divorces, we should never feel true shame about who we are as God's cherished creatures.

You may have made mistakes, but he never sees you as a mistake.

You may have failed, but in God's eyes you are never a failure.

You may have behaved atrociously, but in his eyes you are not atrocious.

You're just like the rest of us—human and weak, but never alone; passionately pursued by God and deeply, tenderly loved. Do you believe that?

Take Your Emotional X ray *Lord, what is blocking my heart from knowing, trusting, or feeling—despite how I fail—how precious I am in your eyes? Remove it, please!*

Loneliness

We Interrupt This Program

My husband and I had tried desperately to have a baby, but three operations and thousands of dollars later I found out that I could never carry a child to full term. After that I cried when I saw mothers with precious little newborns, and for years I even avoided going to baby showers. It was too painful. Following my divorce, I not only had no children, but I had no husband and no home of my own. Deep loneliness set in. I became emotionally stuck on what I wanted and did not currently have.

One lonely night I grabbed a handful of chocolate chips out of the Toll House bag, threw myself onto the sofa, and turned on the television. Feeling like I would be alone forever, I was suddenly aware of God trying to speak to me over the blare of the commercials. Thankfully I've disciplined myself to stop when those thoughts come, in case it's God trying to get through. I became still and listened as my heart and head were moved with the words, "Do you really think I, the One who loves you more than anything and who knows what you need, would never let you have love again in your life?"

In that moment I knew that in response to my deepest desires for love God would always bring me someone who would love me and whom I could love: a niece, a friend, a coworker. His timing is perfect. I just had to quit focusing on some imagined Prince Charming and trust that the King would grant my wishes in his way and his time. Can you do the same?

Daily Dose of God's Word "Delight yourself in the Lord and he will give you the desires of your heart." (Ps. 37:4)

Hungry for Love

My friend Bradley James is an accomplished musician, composer, and singer. He was privileged to work closely with Mother Teresa for eleven years, and before she died, she gave him exclusive rights to put her words and prayers to music. I love to hear his stories of how simply and sweetly Mother Teresa tended to the lowliest, and often most lonesome, of God's children.

"Mother traveled around the world and spoke to many affluent crowds," Bradley reminded me one day. "She told all who would listen that we are all called to be missionaries, but we don't need to go to Calcutta or even to leave our own homes to be effective."

"What do you mean?" I asked Bradley.

"She said we're called first to feed those who are starving for love and to minister to those who are poor in spirit. She said Calcutta was right here; the poor and hungry are in our own homes."

The little saint was right. *The poor and hungry are in our own homes.* Having been though a miserable marriage and a painful divorce myself, I know the hunger for love and poverty of spirit that loneliness brings. If you are lonely and starving for love, ask God to feed you with healthy friendships, and trust he will multiply whatever small love you have in your life to abundance.

Daily Dose of God's Word   "When he had taken the seven loaves and given thanks, he broke them and gave them to his disciples to set before the people, and they did so. . . . The people ate and were satisfied." (Mark 8:6–8)

Reach Out and Touch Someone

I was deeply moved when I watched the documentary about Mother Teresa and her missionaries. With veils pinned back and sleeves rolled up, the nuns scurried busily about the hospital ward tending to various medical needs of the sick children. One emaciated, brown-skinned boy lay curled in a fetal position in the whitewashed crib when the slender sister approached him. While his eyes gazed blankly into space, she bent down toward him, scooped her arm beneath his head, and lifted him slightly. His eyes darted furtively, and like a frightened animal, he began to twitch nervously. I watched to see if she was going to feed him, or give him medicine or some other medical treatment. What she gave him surprised me.

The young nurse began to rub the boy's chest with firm, circular strokes. She broadened her strokes to include his shoulders and neck, and back down around his heart. Her capable hands moved up over his face, around his scalp and neck, and back down to his chest. Quietly and faithfully she worked her repetitive touch on his frail body.

Slowly his twitching stopped, his body relaxed, and the darting eyes moved to her face and stayed there. As his eyes locked on hers, I saw the connection between them and the powerful healing of physical touch. Breaking his isolation and loneliness, the young woman's loving hands brought the patient from panic to peace.

Band-Aid for Your Soul If you're lonely, make sure you're getting healthy human touch. Get a manicure or therapeutic massage. Touch your kids. Hug your friends. Hold hands with your parents.

Keep Watch with Me

It was the night he was betrayed. Jesus had just celebrated the Passover meal with his disciples in the Upper Room, where he'd said someone in the room was going to betray him. Judas had taken off, and Peter was swearing up and down he'd never betray his Master. Minds were confused, emotions were high, and the mood was surely tense. After this Last Supper, the group walked up the Mount of Olives to the Garden of Gethsemane. Telling the others to stay while he went off a short distance to pray, Jesus took Peter, James, and John with him and confided, "My soul is overwhelmed with sorrow to the point of death. Stay here and keep watch with me" (Matt. 26:38).

Jesus was feeling the weight of what lay ahead and did not want to be alone. He was counting on his friends to be with him. But three times his friends fell asleep and failed to give him the emotional comfort and support he needed. Have you ever felt that lonely?

Good friends are a blessing. They can help us through tough times, and their love and encouragement can see us through dark nights. After divorce, we need good friends, but we also need to remember they're not perfect. Our family, friends, and children have lives of their own. There will be times they can't, or even won't, be there for us when we feel lonely.

Jesus may have felt abandoned by his friends, but Luke's gospel tells us God sent an angel to minister to him in the garden when he needed it most, and he will send you comfort when you need it most too.

Take Your Emotional Temperature *Lord, sometimes I get so lonely I feel like I could sweat blood. Help me to remember I'm never really alone, but you are with me and will comfort me.*

It Never Lasts Forever

Gina had just broken off her first significant dating relationship since her divorce. She emailed me a graphic description of her feelings of loneliness.

"I had the worst attack of loneliness this weekend. It was torturous. The volcano erupted, the tidal wave and earthquake hit, and an all-time heartbreak has sent me reeling out of control. After hours and hours of crying, I'm at my end. I just can't do this alone. I'm forty-four years old and have no partner, no kids, no significant other, no significant family (except my mom), and no single friends. Everyone is married—everyone! I'm sick of eating alone, sleeping alone, and being alone. I'm scared and frightened and not sane anymore."

Gina's feelings are not uncommon. Loneliness can consume us if we don't know how to manage our emotions. After my divorce I felt the same way Gina did, and the worst part was that I feared the loneliness would last forever. But does loneliness ever last forever? Don't we tend to exaggerate the possibility in our minds? Remember that fear is usually at the root of our negative emotions. Remember, too, that fear reflects a lack of faith.

How can you combat loneliness? The best way is to move out of the isolation, help someone else, volunteer, meet with friends, or spend time with relatives. Sometimes, though, you have no opportunity to make human connections, and you just have to wait it out. That's where your faith can conquer fear.

Doctor's Rx Close your eyes right now and reflect on the reality that no matter who is out of your life, for however long you'll be "alone," a loving, caring God is always with you.

Rejection

He'll Never Forsake You

Divorce is the ultimate rejection.

The person who once loved you and pledged to live with you "til death do us part" has either walked out on you or has refused to honor you or the marriage relationship so that you felt compelled to leave. Either way, you were rejected.

The person with whom you became one flesh, with whom you may have borne children, with whom you shared your home, your life, and your heart has shattered your dreams and broken your heart.

Rejection screams you weren't worthy enough for your spouse to do whatever it would have taken to make the marriage work. Rejection coldheartedly declares that while your husband or wife may have genuinely loved you, he or she obviously now loves something or someone else . . . *more*. Rejection charges that you didn't measure up. You weren't worth the effort, the sacrifice, or their hanging in for the long haul.

Are you feeling rejected? Rejection is an emotional poison that makes you feel heavy and dull. Do you want the antidote? Remember who loves you as if you were the only person on earth. He is the One who not only thinks you are worth the effort, but who will never give up pursuing you passionately. He would even die for you . . . and in fact did.

Physical Therapy Relax and slowly take a deep breath and then slowly exhale. Repeat. Imagine breathing in God's grace. Exhale rejection; inhale love. Exhale rejection; inhale love. Practice daily.

Little Gods Everywhere

When I was little, I adored my mom and dad. Even though they began to teach me about God at an early age, my parents were my god. They were the ones who made me feel loved, protected, and secure. They took care of me in every way. I wanted to please my parents so they'd continue loving me, approving of me, and, of course, feeding me!

Then I went to grade school where I had strict but loving teachers. I performed as best I could to please my teachers because I wanted their love and approval. I also wanted those good grades. In the classroom and on the playground I met kids who were cool, and I wanted to fit in with them. I wanted their approval in order to validate how okay I was. If they accepted me, that would make me cool too.

What came next? Boys! Tall ones, cute ones, strong ones, smart ones. I loved them all and hoped they all loved me! I began to walk, talk, dress, and behave in ways that I thought would gain their approval, love, and loyalty.

What I was doing was adding to my list of false gods—persons in whom I sought my identity, self-worth, security, and love. Despite the genuine good I gained from my human relationships, every one of them let me down in some way or rejected me. And I let them down too or rejected them, sometimes knowingly, sometimes unawares.

Heart Pill It may be hard to swallow, but there is only ONE love that will never fail. After your dreams and hopes have been dashed by a divorce, can you remember that? What keeps you still pursuing perfect love from imperfect people?

Insulated, Not Isolated

So, just because people aren't perfect, does that mean we should give up our desire for relationships with them? No, but we should give up our desire to get all our needs met through others.

Rejection happens to everyone. Instead of furiously performing to avoid rejection, we can learn to handle it. Dr. Gary Lawrence, a Christian counselor in the Phoenix, Arizona area, specializes in rejection issues. He says most of us "tap-dance on the tables of life" in order to avoid rejection. He told me, "Instead of *isolating* ourselves from people, places, or things that might hurt us, we should be *insulating* ourselves from rejection."

Dr. Lawrence shared a story about a woman he'd counseled who had been divorced and stayed isolated from new relationships because she feared rejection. "Rejection kept her a prisoner in her own home," Dr. Lawrence explained. "She also avoided talking to her ex-husband about the kids because she feared he would reject her ideas, thoughts, or concerns as he had done in their marriage. Fear of rejection kept her from communicating important information about the children with their father. Everything she did, or didn't do, was to avoid rejection."

After divorce, we can still fear rejection from our ex, our kids, our friends, the courts, and even the church. Tap dancing on other people's tables puts a strain on our hearts!

Take Your Emotional Temperature Is avoiding rejection imprisoning me? *Lord, when I find fear of rejection controlling me, I need to remind myself to value your love and approval rather than that of others. Help me unplug from their power source and into yours.*

The Rejection Connection

If we look at Jesus' life, we can learn how to handle rejection. Jesus' own neighbors ran him out of Nazareth. He preached with the kindest love, the purest heart, and the strongest truth, yet people still didn't listen. The crowds challenged him, the Pharisees tried to trick him, and the Jewish leaders even sentenced him to a barbaric crucifixion. Stripped, spat upon, pricked with thorns, publicly humiliated, and nailed to a cross, Jesus didn't just die—he also endured endless emotional pain and rejection. His actual physical death may have been the least painful part.

When the people rejected his teaching, Jesus maintained emotional balance by spending time with friends and time alone in prayer. When Judas and the high priests rejected him, he spent time in prayer with his Father. On the cross, he still stayed connected in prayer with the Father, crying out at times, but never forgetting who he was and why he was there. Scripture tells us, "During the days of Jesus' life on earth, he offered up prayers and petitions with loud cries and tears to the one who could save him from death, and he was heard because of his reverent submission" (Heb. 5:7).

Jesus didn't invite rejection, but neither did he avoid it when it came.

Doctor's Rx To handle rejection, especially through divorce, don't pretend you're untouched or unhurt by it. Call out "in loud cries and tears" but fix your eyes on the Father and remind yourself of who you are in him and how deeply you are loved.

Fear

Lions and Tigers and Dentists . . . Oh No!

My spiritual advisor is a godly man, a sinner like me, but a little older and a lot further along than I am in the spiritual journey. I value his experience and insight evidenced by the most appropriate homework he always sends me home with after our sessions. After one session he assigned my spiritual exercise for the month: keep a written list of all my fears. "Write down fears that don't even seem spiritual. Like the fear of going to the dentist," he said.

I cringed. How did he know? When I was six, Dr. Worsely slapped me because I was squirming too much in the dental chair, and for years I dreaded going to the dentist. I wondered if my advisor could see inside the deepest recesses of my mind and expose other hidden fears like black widow spiders, giant cockroaches, fast rides at the fair, and—oh no, more cellulite.

I never realized how much fear controlled me until I wrote it all out on paper: Fear of not being loved, fear of failing, and fear of being abandoned were some of my biggest fears. In my head I know I'm loved, it's okay if I fail, and God will never abandon me. But I don't always feel what I know about God and life and love.

Does what you believe in your head always ring true with the wild emotions in your heart? Do you have complete faith in God, or do you still struggle with emotional or irrational fears? You might think you have very few fears, but I bet you have lots. Like me.

Take Your Emotional X ray Make your own fear list— be honest. Keep it around for a few weeks and watch it grow. Then make a list of all the things, people, or events you used to fear that have not materialized or that God has given you peace about.

47

Think You're Not Afraid?

If you have written a list of your fears, you might begin to realize that all fears can be boiled down to a few greater underlying fears that are basic to all mankind: rejection, loss of self-worth or identity, and loss of control. Notice where these typical post-divorce fears fit those basic categories:

- Fear that your children will feel more loyalty to the other parent is a *fear of rejection.*
- Fear of not having a new lover after divorce, especially if you rely on relationships and sex to define your value, is a *fear of loss of self-worth.*
- Not wanting to compromise in the custody or visitation agreement is *fear of losing control.*

When Adam and Eve sinned and were locked out of Eden, they felt rejection. In their guilt they lost their feelings of self-worth and felt ashamed; they lost dominion over creation and must have felt loss of control. Those three basic desires, acceptance (love), self-worth, and control—and the fear of losing them—drive us all.

Since your divorce, do you find some of these fears driving you? What fears are blocking your heart from giving and receiving love, worth, and freedom?

Doctor's Rx Today spend some time trying to identify the greatest emotional fear you have. Ask God to reveal through his Word how you can replace that fear with faith. Don't forget to spend quiet time listening for the answer.

Facing Fears Is Freedom

Jesse was afraid he'd lose the right to see his sons. Three years following their divorce, Jesse's ex-wife was repeatedly threatening to take away their two boys. When Jesse didn't cooperate with her on some minor issue, she'd file a restraining order against him, claiming he had verbally or otherwise abused the children. While Jesse tried to teach his sons responsibility, their mother continued to coddle them. In and out of the courts, Jesse spent thousands of dollars trying to restore his visitation rights.

Jesse feared his ex-wife, feared losing more money, and feared defending himself against more false accusations. The latest drama was an accusation of physical abuse. Learning to work the system, the boys would report to overprotective Mom that Dad was "mean" since he made them do chores and would not let them eat dinner or go to bed until they were finished. Afraid to exercise his God-given authority over his boys, Jesse became increasingly angry and depressed. Fear fed the anger; anger fed the depression. Jesse was caught in an emotionally destructive cycle until he learned how to stop feeding his fear, the source of his negative emotions.

He told me, "I remembered God's words that he would work all things out, in his way, in his time. I let go of the fear and replaced it with faith that even if I lost the boys, God would somehow restore them to me in the future. I even dared to face that maybe future restoration would not happen, and that I needed to be okay with that, too. When I refused to live in fear and was willing to accept the worst, I was free."

Daily Dose of God's Word   "Cast all your anxiety on him because he cares for you." (I Pet. 5:7)

49

Even the Faithful Are Fearful

Jesus experienced fear too.

Imagine if Jesus had not feared the whip on his flesh, the thorns on his head, or the nails in his hands and feet. He would have been cool, calm, and collected, going off to his death like it was some Friday afternoon business meeting that would close the deal on salvation. But Jesus, who was both God and man, feared pain as we do. The stress, which is just another form of fear, began to get to Jesus right after the Last Supper. Even though all four gospels tell of the time Jesus prayed in the garden, it's the physician, Luke, who described a physical detail of Jesus' fear of death. While Jesus begged his Father to remove the suffering, we're told, "His sweat was like drops of blood falling to the ground" (Luke 22:44). Now that's fear!

We're so afraid of admitting we're afraid. We think fear makes us weak and cowardly, when actually it only means we're human. Sometimes it's smart to be afraid when we're staying on guard against some potential evil. Intelligent fear, like anger, can be a normal human response, as it was with Jesus. It's when we nurse fear that we get into trouble. We invite it in, sit it down, and mentally and emotionally feed it until it gets so big and bloated it controls our lives. Have you had physical symptoms of fear? Do you lose sleep worrying about money? Have you had headaches, backaches, or a queasy stomach because you were afraid to face your ex-spouse? Have you sweated blood?

Daily Dose of God's Word "Be on your guard; stand firm in the faith; be men of courage; be strong. Do everything in love." (1 Cor. 16:13, 14)

Bitterness

Got Root Rot?

Sweet-smelling grasses and pungent pine trees grow thick and green in the breathtakingly beautiful lakeside forests of Michigan's Upper Peninsula. No one would suspect that lurking just below the surface of this postcard-pretty picture is the giant, life-sucking armillaria bulbosa fungus, one of the world's largest living organisms. The 1,500-year-old fungus covers over thirty-seven acres (more than five football fields), weighs in excess of a hundred tons (the weight of about fifty cars), and is described by botanists as "roughly the texture of rotting fabric." Most of the fungus lives underground, but tree-rot and mushroom growth are visible signs on the surface.

Bitterness hides much the same way in our lives. We may be professionally coifed, manicured, and fit, with perfect church attendance and beautiful clothes with shoes to match. We might be fierce prayer warriors, hard workers, wonderful parents, friends, or selfless volunteers, but just beneath the surface hides the rotting root of bitterness. Bitterness can take the form of anger, self-pity, general irritability, anxiety, or feelings of hopelessness.

Like a fungus that eventually takes over and kills its host, the bitterness we harbor as a result of our divorces can invade and destroy our emotional, physical, and spiritual health. Our problems that we might think are isolated or unrelated to our divorces can actually be symptoms of a giant root of bitterness. Are you harboring resentments beneath your surface? They're keeping you from being the most beautiful and healthy creation God intended.

Take Your Emotional X ray *Lord, I want to be free of emotional root-rot. Will you show me the areas in which I need to replace my spiritual fungus with faith?*

Look Before You Bite!

What does bitterness look like? A ripe, juicy apple might have a bruise, a worm, or a fungus. While the three are different, each is an invader and ultimately a destroyer of the ripe fruit's flesh. Emotional bitterness may also take different forms. It is any negative attitude that robs us of the sweetness of life as God intended. It can appear noble, self-sacrificing, or even just. It can look like anger, depression, fear, resentment, or a wounded spirit. No matter the type of bitterness, it's all spiritually destructive.

The anxious single mother who works herself to death all day, worries constantly about the bills, still tries to get her children to every sports or school activity despite the lack of money or time, is bitter. She hasn't let go, or taught her children to let go, of the things that are just too much for them to handle in this season of their lives. As a result, she, and the children, are always wired or tired.

The noncustodial father who resents having to pay more than 30 percent of his paycheck to his newly remarried and now financially well-off ex-wife is bitter. The man who gets along just fine with his ex-wife but jokingly refers to her as "Hitler" is bitter. The woman who refuses to go to the hospital to see her first grandchild because her ex-husband's wife will be there is bitter.

Bitterness blocks us from receiving God's grace. Are there any areas of your life where your attitude is less than sweet?

Daily Dose of God's Word "Get rid of all bitterness, rage and anger, brawling and slander, along with every form of malice." (Eph. 4:31)

Sweet and Sour

A friend I've known for years came to Palm Desert to visit me for a few days. One evening while he was here, we drove down Shadow Mountain Drive to get to Sullivan's, a favorite restaurant that served icy cold drinks and sizzling steaks on a beautiful brick patio. As we pulled up to the restaurant, I pointed out the house across the street where my ex-husband lived. "That's his house," I said casually, as we pulled into the restaurant parking lot.

The next day we made a run to the grocery store and as we passed my ex's home, I saw his truck in the driveway. "There's his truck," I mentioned in passing.

The next day we were cruising down the same street when I saw my ex-husband's girlfriend's car parked next to his. "Gee, his girlfriend must be there," I muttered under my breath.

My friend, who loves me dearly and never minces words, said, "Rose, do you realize you say something every time we pass his house?"

I stopped. He was right. Not that I otherwise thought about my ex, but when I drove by, my focus was always fixed on my ex and what was going on in his life. I didn't want to admit that after all these years I was still—gulp—bitter! A little or a lot, bitterness leaves a bad taste in your mouth. Are you still bitter about something or someone?

Doctor's Rx For bitterness, take three teaspoons of sugar: forgiveness, acceptance, and love.

Numbing the Pain

Numb Can Be Dumb

When our hearts hurt, especially from divorce, most of us run out and eat, buy, or do something else to numb the pain. It's normal to want to ease pain and suffering, but sometimes we indulge too much and end up paying an unpleasant price. Have you ever had a double dose of Novocain at the dentist? Sure it blocks the pain, but for the next few hours one side of your face sags like a Salvador Dali painting, cheeks drooped down, and a steady stream of drool falling to the floor. "Ga-ga-ga," is about all you can say, and you can't smile, drink, or eat. What good is that?

Have you ever tried to talk after eating a huge bowl of ice cream? Sometimes when I treat myself to a freezing cold chocolate-and-peanut-butter yogurt at the local ice cream parlor, my tongue gets numb and can barely move. My mouth loves the taste, but afterward I can't form simple speech. "That wath really delithiouth! May I pleathe have two mediumth to go?"

The pain we feel after divorce calls for numbing, but we need to be careful about the aftereffects of too much emotional Novocain. The pursuit of pleasure to avoid pain can come back around and cause much more suffering for us in the end.

What have you been using to numb the pain in your life? Sleep? Spending? Overworking or performing? Do you escape into television, eating, dating, sex, or the internet?

Take a Heart Pill If you are trying to self-medicate, try a quiet time in prayer, listening to beautiful music, good reading, or other balanced pleasures that brings you closer to God.

Quick Fixes or Slow Deaths?

 Recently at a luncheon I sat next to a young grandmother who told me of her daughter's divorce.

"Emily has always had emotional problems. When she was eighteen I talked her into getting married because she was pregnant. I figured they could work it out. I was wrong. Then I talked her into getting a divorce. Now I'm sorry I did that because she came over one day, dropped the kids off, and told me to take them because she couldn't handle being a single mother."

"Wow," I said sympathetically, "Where are the kids now?"

She looked relieved. "She's moved in with a man and feels strong enough now to take the kids back." Sensing my disapproval, she added, "It's good. She needs to be in another relationship. She was in too much pain. She's one of those people who just can't be alone."

I wanted to scream at the top of my lungs, "NO! You're WRONG! She does NOT need to be in another relationship right now!" But I kept my mouth shut. Grandma wasn't ready to hear the truth. She'd obviously sheltered her daughter from pain for so long the poor girl never grew up. Her daughter is addicted to the quick-fix of relationships to help her avoid the pain of maturity. Have you ever sought a quick fix to avoid the lesson that trials or suffering teach?

Daily Dose of God's Word "No discipline seems pleasant at the time, but painful. Later on, however, it produces a harvest of righteousness and peace for those who have been trained by it." (Heb. 12:11)

Now and Later

 Too much shopping can be fun, but not when we blow our budgets.

Too much eating of our favorite foods helps us feel better for the moment, but we pay the price when we gain weight and threaten our health.

Too much partying might seem exciting, but not when we can get entangled in unhealthy relationships.

Too much sleeping is restful, but not when we use it to escape what needs to be done.

Too much time spent in an enjoyable hobby can turn into an addictive avoidance.

It's funny how we declare "No pain, no gain" when it comes to sports, bodybuilding, competition, or other achievements. Many of us are willing to suffer now for the big payoff later. We diet for the class reunion, save and scrimp for the big vacation, and run the extra mile for the extra muscle. Why don't we embrace pain or suffering for emotional or spiritual rewards?

Maybe after divorce we don't think there's ever going to be a future reward worth some sacrifice. Without hope, and weary of pain, we settle for pursuit of immediate pleasure. Have we forgotten God's promises for us?

Daily Dose of God's Word "But those who hope in the LORD will renew their strength. They will soar on wings like eagles; they will run and not grow weary, they will walk and not be faint." (Isa. 40:31)

Fast Track to Heart Attack

God's design of the cardiovascular system displays his genius. The heart, blood, and blood vessels transport oxygen and nutrients to the cells while efficiently removing waste products. About every thirty seconds your heart pumps your five liters of blood through your sixty thousand miles of arteries and veins.

What happens, though, when you gain weight? When you add one pound—equivalent to those four sticks of butter in your refrigerator—you grow *four hundred more miles* of blood vessels. As a result, your heart works harder, rests less, and moves more quickly to the end of its life.

Your emotional and spiritual heart works somewhat the same way. When you add more work, more activity, more noise, more friendships, more commitments, and more achievements to an already overloaded emotional life, you move your heart closer to death. The extra weight you add, hoping to stay busy and avoid the lingering pain of divorce, also keeps you separated from time spent with God, talking to him, listening to him, and just being in his presence.

God designed your emotional heart to seek him for rest, peace, and relief from pain. Are your choices of numbing activities interfering with his grand design?

Today's Treatment Turn off your cell phone. Listen to the quiet instead of the car radio, even if it's inspirational music. Ask God to show you the overweight areas in your life. Which one comes to mind that you can start changing today?

How Do You Spell R-E-L-I-E-F?

Have you ever watched open-heart surgery on television or in real life? It's gruesome and awesome at the same time.

The doctor slices into the chest with a sharp scalpel and deftly pulls aside the flesh and muscle to expose the rib cage and the heart lying safely beneath the bones. In order to get to the heart the surgeon uses a high powered instrument to saw through ribs. Can you imagine the pain if you were the patient . . . and awake? Thankfully the anesthesiologist administers just the right dose of medication to numb the pain.

Persistent pain demands relief. Even Jesus sought relief from suffering when he called out to his Father in the Garden of Gethsemane or when he went away by himself for a time to pray. The key to keeping perspective on emotional pain is to look for and heal the real heart of the problem and not to overdose on "painkillers" in the interim.

Are you ready to ask God to reveal the heart of your emotional struggle? It may not be what you assume. Trouble at work, with your ex, or with the kids may only be the symptoms, not the heart, of what ails you. God may be at work sawing through your self-protective rib cage in order to expose your heart. Seeking relief from the pain is normal, but make sure you administer just the right kind and level of medication!

Physical Therapy Make a list of any ways you have been over-medicating: sleep, work, eating, or other normal-but-now-addictive behaviors. What can you substitute that is healthier for you? What negative thinking is keeping you stuck?

Grief

Creative Memories

Have your eyes ever been so puffy and swollen from crying they looked like freshly cut slits in rising dough? Mine have. It happened the week I finally surrendered to the fullness of my grief about losing my husband and my stepson.

On a Saturday morning I took the phone off the hook, put on a fresh pot of Starbucks coffee, and pulled out five shoeboxes full of family photos. I decided to make a picture album of the last ten years of our life, celebrating the genuine love and joy we'd had. When I finished I wanted to give it to my stepson so he'd always have a tangible reminder that his father and I had loved each other, and that I especially had loved him.

I spent that weekend and the next few days alternating between laughing out loud and weeping silently. Deep, mournful, gushing tears. No holding back, I let them come. I honored my grief without guilt or regret.

A week later I gave the album, one family's life and my dreams preserved between plastic pages, to my ex-husband and stepson. When I gave it to them, we all cried and had one last "family" hug. It was an affirming, cleansing ritual of release for me.

Doctor's Rx Rituals are helpful in closing the door on pain so that we can move on in love and joy. Preserving photos, giving away old memorabilia, or having a good-bye dinner might work for some. Can you think of something you can do to face and embrace your grief in a healthy way?

Washed with Tears

 Each person's grief is unique, but everyone's grief is the same.

In divorce we all experience the death of our dreams and hopes for the future. Even if you left an abusive relationship and things are better now, you probably suffered many types of losses, and perhaps still do. The whole grief process includes initial shock, denial, anger, guilt, bargaining, depression, release, acceptance, and finally recovery. However, the order in which we go through the stages and the timing and intensity will vary for each of us. Feelings of grief can come and go . . . and come again when we least expect them.

Have you ever been ambushed by grief—tears that came when you least expected them?

The stage of grieving where we weep and wail over our losses can also be called the bereavement or mourning period. When I made the photo album, I was in death-like bereavement, mourning the loss of all that I'd held dear. It was a necessary and normal path of healing that my emotions automatically took since I had not tried to shove them down.

We know God created a system of healing for our physical bodies. Why do we forget he also created a system of healing for our minds and emotions? Mourning is a self-limiting, emotionally cleansing, and healing process. Try to prevent it or stop it and you will eventually hurt even more. So let it out—the pain will come, but so will the healing.

Take Your Emotional Temperature *Father, I don't like to grieve. It's sad, painful, and drains me of energy. Help me see that you created grief to help me heal.*

63

A Night of Weeping

Grief is agonizing. Grief is overpowering. Grief is normal. Grief will always be a part of your life, but you don't have to let it control you.

Grief can sneak up and overtake you unless you turn to face it and embrace it. To get beyond grief you must go through it, not around it. You can't do your grief work in isolation. You'll need someone to listen.

Grief comes in waves. Some waves are bigger than others, but if you learn how to ride them out in healthy ways, they will get smaller over time.

Grief's duration and intensity are not necessarily tied to the number of years you were married. Some people with shorter marriages will experience deeper grieving than those with longer ones.

Grief after second or third marriages can be more intense because of the extra feelings of failure and diminished hope for future success.

Grief can be interrupted by other tragedies and may have to be revisited in the future.

The good news—grief doesn't last forever.

Daily Dose of God's Word "Sing to the LORD, you saints of his; praise his holy name. For his anger lasts only a moment, but his favor lasts a lifetime; weeping may remain for a night, but rejoicing comes in the morning." (Ps. 30:4, 5)

The Four "R's"

Do you need some helpful methods to get through grief?

Receive the Truth: Admit the reality of all aspects of your situation. Say it out loud and talk about it as much or as often as you need with a trusted friend, family member, or support group. Involve the kids only at appropriate age levels to teach them a healthy mourning process.

Recall the Loss: Talking about it is only the first step. Too often we stay stuck at the cognitive level of reality, trying to keep our emotions under control. Revisit the past as a part of the healing process; let yourself remember, imagine, look at old photos, play the old music, pack up the old things, and recall warm memories. Cry, get mad, and then cry again. Pray for release and peace.

Release the Past: Make sure you've allowed yourself sufficient time for crying or otherwise getting your emotions out. When you think you're ready for it, ritual is a good way of releasing. Thank God for what was good.

Reinvest Yourself: Mourning requires large amounts of energy. When you've received the truth, recalled the loss, and released the past, you'll have much more time and energy to reinvest yourself with God, your family, your friends, and your community.

Daily Dose of God's Word "God is our refuge and strength, an ever-present help in trouble. Therefore we will not fear, though the earth give way and the mountains fall into the heart of the sea." (Ps 46:1, 2)

You Deserve a Break Today

Sometimes our emotions are like kids cooped up in the car on a day-long drive to Disneyland. After just a few hours, our children can be so wound up that we can't concentrate on where we are driving. Have you ever tried to focus on the freeway but found yourself screaming louder and more frequently for them to settle down and be quiet? Any mom or dad knows what happens next: unless you want to go insane and drive into oncoming traffic and kill everyone, you have to pull over for a break.

The doors fly open and kids scramble out and head for the restroom or snack machine. When energy, noise, and tension escalate, wise parents know to stop and let the kids out to eat, run hard, and play. After children have been given room to release those energies in a controlled, safe environment, they'll crawl back into the car and fall asleep while you continue to cruise contentedly on your trip.

Some likely pent-up emotions, especially post-divorce, are worry, fear, anxiety, anger, depression, loneliness, and hurt. Our feelings, right or wrong, have their own energy force. If we don't control them and let them out in a safe environment, the energy that's stuffed inside will cause us to crash emotionally or physically. And we never know who else on life's highway, even those near and dear to us, will be involved in our suffering

Doctor's Rx Take a break today if you need it, no matter where you are or what you're doing. Begin to listen to your body, become more in tune with oncoming stress, anger, or tears, and pull over for an emotional pit stop. Your "kids" will thank you for it.

Forgiveness

Let Go and Let God

Sara's ex-husband cheated on her and during their divorce proceedings he lied to the court about his income. Three years after their divorce, the thought of her ex-spouse still made Sara miserable. "I put him through school and raised his children. No one has ever betrayed me more than Joe."

Sara asked me to help her understand why she was still struggling emotionally from her divorce. "My attorney negotiated a good settlement, the kids seem to be stable, and I really like my job. I'm feeling better about myself and even lost some weight. Some nice men have asked me out. I should be happy, but I'm not. What's wrong?"

When I suggested maybe she hadn't forgiven her husband, she cut me off. "No way! I told him I forgave him. We talked. I've prayed about it. I *know* I've forgiven him."

"Forgiveness doesn't happen in our heads, Sara," I said. "It happens in our hearts. Talking about it is a good start, but total forgiveness is a conscious decision to let go of the offense. It's willing, not reluctant. When you focus on the fact that no one ever betrayed you more than your ex, you're giving me a hint about where your heart is. You're right . . . no one has ever betrayed you more, but isn't that between Joe and God now?"

"Well, how will I know when I've really forgiven him?" she asked.

"When you quit focusing on how much he hurt you. When you decide to let God take care of what he did."

Take Your Emotional Temperature Is unforgiveness still eating at you? Remember, harboring bitterness is like you're taking poison and hoping the betrayer gets sick or dies.

Who's in Control Here?

 In our talk about her emotional struggles, Sara challenged me about forgiveness.

"I guess the reason I can't forgive my ex-husband is that what he did was wrong. I don't want to seem like I approve or that it didn't bother me or that he can just be let off the hook. I don't want him to think he got away with it. I can't trust him, and I refuse to pretend it didn't happen," she said.

"Sara, you don't have to accept it at all," I advised her. "No one should ever tolerate infidelity or lies, and you certainly don't have to make excuses for him. You also don't have to trust him or even like him, *but you do have to love him.* Real love isn't a romantic or friendly feeling. It means releasing him to God and getting rid of your own bitterness toward him. Get your focus off his actions and back onto your attitude. Can you do that?"

"I want to, but it's hard," she said. "I keep thinking about what he did, and it makes me so mad!"

"Then capture your thoughts, Sara. Either you control them or they control you."

Daily Dose of God's Word "Finally, brothers, whatever is true, whatever is noble, whatever is right, whatever is pure, whatever is lovely, whatever is admirable—if anything is excellent or praise-worthy—think about such things. Whatever you have learned or received or heard from me, or seen in me—put it into practice. And the God of peace will be with you." (Phil. 4:8, 9)

69

The Good News

What forgiveness is NOT:

It's not approving of what the other person did. You have the right, and often the responsibility, to express disapproval of wrongdoing.

It's not accepting what the other person did. You don't have to tolerate improper or sinful behavior or attitudes. In fact if you do, you become party to the problem.

It's not excusing or justifying the other person's behavior. You don't always have to find or make up reasons why your ex did what he or she did that hurt you.

It's not staying friendly with the other person. If someone continually lies, hurts, or abuses you, you don't have to be his or her friend. Jesus told his disciples to shake the dust off their feet and leave town when people rejected them. And he didn't insist they become buddies with the Pharisees.

It's not forgetting. Remembering helps you stay safe, but you should tuck the memory away and keep your focus on whatever is good.

It's not continuing to trust the other person. You are not obligated to trust anyone. In fact, sometimes that's stupid, or worse . . . dangerous. Trust and respect have to be earned. We can't always trust man, but we can always trust God.

Doctor's Rx Make a list of everyone who has hurt you and begin to pray for the gift of God's grace to truly, fully, and finally forgive.

Fear Again?

What forgiveness IS:

It's seeing the other person through Jesus' eyes. He sees all the flaws and loves that person anyway. Are you a better judge than Jesus?

It's trusting God to take care of justice. You might withhold forgiveness because you don't believe God will deal with the hurtful person properly. You may want to punish him or her since you don't think God will. Or you don't think he will act soon enough for you!

It's releasing the hurt in your own heart. Holding on to unforgiveness keeps you stuck at the greatest point of your pain. Forgiving takes the needle out of your own heart.

It's choosing to obey God. Regardless of how you feel, or all the reasons and rationalizations why you should or shouldn't forgive, God commands it. If you love him, you will keep his commandments. It's that simple.

It's opening the door to receiving forgiveness from God for your own sins. Scripture says that if you don't forgive, you make it impossible for God to forgive you. Remember, "Forgive us our debts, as we also have forgiven our debtors"? The "as" means *just like.* God will forgive us *just like* we forgive others. That means if we don't, he can't either.

Take Your Emotional Temperature What fears are keeping you from forgiving someone who hurt you?

Through the Looking Glass

Although the Twelve Step program of Alcoholics Anonymous was originally designed in the 1930s to help alcoholics overcome their drinking problems, it has evolved into a philosophy and a way of life that tries to help people become all that God intended. As Christians we know that working the steps in any recovery program relies on a total surrender to, and childlike dependence on, God through his Son, Jesus Christ. In that light, I think Step Four can help us look at forgiveness from another perspective:

Step Four—We made a searching, fearless moral inventory of ourselves.

How many of us have ever done that? Have you ever written a list of every time you lied, cheated, were mean, nasty, snotty, selfish, rude, arrogant, prideful, deceptive, unkind, uncaring, gossipy, lustful, or disobedient? Has your focus been so long on the other person that you've forgotten your own flaws? Looking honestly at yourself helps you see others as Christ sees them—just like you!

This fourth step is not new; Jesus cautioned his listeners, "Why do you look at the speck of sawdust in your brother's eye and pay no attention to the plank in your own eye?" (Matt. 7:3). That means taking your own inventory first. Jesus also taught that despite our sins we are loved and can be forgiven. If he so deeply loves that person who hurt you, how can you continue to withhold forgiveness from him or her?

Doctor's Rx Go to a quiet place, ask for grace, and make a thorough examination of conscience. Confess your sins and receive God's forgiveness and grace. Then meditate on how deeply and passionately you are loved despite your sins.

Lemons or Lemonade?

Spring arrived in the desert with sunny skies and a bounty of new buds on my lemon tree. Warmed during the day, the tree sends out the heady scent of citrus blossoms into the cool evening and through my open windows at night. I might dream of sugar plums in the winter, but this time of year it's lemon meringue pie!

Jesus often used stories about fruit and vines to illustrate spiritual truths to those who would listen. Do you know he still does that today? Nature is one of the many ways God continues to reveal himself to us. I went to pluck some fresh lemons the other day and observed two that were next to each other on the same branch. One was plump and shiny, the other much smaller and slightly shriveled. Both had received the same hours of sunshine, amount of watering, and fertilizer in the soil. Something, though, in the smaller feeder branch that attached the shriveled lemon to the main branch had blocked it from receiving necessary nutrients.

Unforgiveness does the same thing to our hearts: It blocks us from receiving God's grace. It also forms a foundation for us to sin more by setting us up to harbor bitterness, to gossip, to be unkind, or even to seek revenge. Unforgiveness also binds us to that person who hurt us. As long as we fail to forgive, they control us! Why extend the misery of divorce by blocking your heart from all the love, joy, and peace that God wants for you?

Band-Aid for Your Soul Buy fresh lemons and make a lemon meringue pie—or lemon bundt cake, pudding, or whatever you like—for dessert. Share this insight with your children or a friend and resolve to bring some spiritual sweetness back into your life.

Why?

What's in My Hair Isn't Fair!

Head lice. They're tough little critters.

When my adopted daughter was eight, every kid in her class came home with a note from the teacher to check for lice. We fought those suckers for weeks until every last one was gone. Recently I went to war again, this time taking on the army of small, white enemies that stuck fiercely to my seven-year-old niece's hair. Hayley, who was staying with me for a week, was in tears at the very thought of her body being invaded by bugs.

Have your kids ever had lice? It's commonly spread in school by sharing combs, hats, hair decorations, and even helmets. Rich kid, poor kids, clean, or dirty . . . no one is immune. You have to wash all the linens and use bug spray on the chairs, couches, car, or other places the children rest their heads. An expensive shampoo will kill the lice but the battle has only begun; you must carefully and thoroughly remove every single egg that has been laid on the hair shaft, or within seven-to-ten days new critters will hatch and take over the head. Then you have to declare war all over again.

Hayley wanted to know why she got lice. She wanted to know *why* she had to endure the embarrassment and torture of getting rid of them. What had she done to deserve this? She thought maybe her friend Brittany was the one who gave them to her. She was looking for a reason and someone to blame. Have you been doing that after your divorce?

Take Your Emotional X ray *Lord, show me why this happened and how I can avoid it in the future. Even though others may have had a part in it, help me not to blame them.*

Wash That Doubt Right Outta Your Hair!

Hayley had to sit with me on the sofa for an hour and a half as I sectioned her lice-ridden hair to carefully run the fine-toothed nit comb through every strand. Her hair is silky and easily tangled, but she patiently endured as I pulled out eggs. I know she hated sitting still and watching me rinse the nits into the pan of water on the coffee table. It wasn't fun, but the repair work was necessary.

Painful repair work after divorce is also necessary. If you're asking yourself why your divorce happened, or why negative things keep happening to you, remember:

Sometimes it's a direct result of your choices. As part of God's natural law, life involves choices and consequences. Divorce is not about God punishing you.

Sometimes you're an innocent victim and have to suffer needlessly. That's also part of life. God never guaranteed total justice, total peace, or total happiness in this life. That all comes in heaven. You can use this pain to develop deeper character, or you can stay bitter.

Sometimes God allows suffering to shape your will to his. There's nothing like suffering to remind you that you're not in control and how much you need God. God will allow you to "suffer" while he works the bugs of compulsions, obsessions, addictions, fears, anxieties, pride, or lust out of your hair. Know that it is a wise, loving hand that works the comb. Be patient.

Physical Therapy Turn your next shampoo into a prayer. While you are working your fingers through your hair, ask God to help you rinse out of your heart whatever is "bugging" you.

Do We Just Want to Control?

Most of us know why we got divorced, but in some cases the reason is not clear. Some people have a persistent, even stubborn, need to know why their divorce happened. Usually such a person was the more optimistic partner, or the one who was in denial about many issues throughout the relationship. Perhaps one spouse was not honest or revealing, and so the other stayed in the dark much of the time, either from naiveté, ignorance, or denial. Because there is no open communication or honesty, a perplexed husband or wife may be left trying to look for clues, frantic to figure it out! What did I do wrong? Who is to blame? Until the answer is found, there is just no peace.

The reason we hate not knowing why is that understanding gives us a sense of control. With control, we can hope to avoid pain and rejection in the future.

- If we understood, we could maybe do something, even now, to save the marriage.
- If we understood, we could change, and then our ex-spouses would love us again.
- If we understood, we could make sure we don't repeat the same mistakes the next time around.

You have a responsibility to understand as much as you can so you can learn from your mistakes, but you may never understand it all. It's fear that can keep us pursuing answers. It's faith that helps us remember answers will be found when we take refuge in him.

Daily Dose of God's Word "As for God, his way is perfect; the word of the Lord is flawless. He is a shield for all who take refuge in him." (Ps. 18:30)

77

God's Sledgehammer

It was a cool, early Saturday morning in 1962 when my little brother, Charlie, and my sister, Barb, and I threw on our jeans, wolfed down some Rice Krispies, and hopped on our Schwinn bicycles. We pedaled down the street, past the cemetery, and into the almond orchard where our neighbor, Mr. Parker, was getting ready to harvest almonds. That day the trees were green and full of fruit.

Mr. Parker was a quiet man with big biceps and a Navy tattoo who drove an old Chevy pickup truck. We watched as he unrolled and shook out a large tarp and laid it down under one slender almond tree whose branches hung heavy with nuts. Then, much to my horror and surprise, Mr. Parker pulled out the biggest sledgehammer I think I've ever seen, told us to step back, and gave the tree a mighty whack!

The tree shook from top to bottom, and in an instant it was raining hundreds of almonds, every branch giving up its fruit. Mr. Parker threw us each a gunnysack, and we scrambled on all fours to gather up the almonds. When I crawled close to see where Mr. Parker had whacked the tree, there was no visible sign of any damage to the trunk, and the tree stood tall and apparently unharmed. Why did you suffer divorce? Maybe it was the "whack" that God wants to use to help you release your grip on things that are not important. With grace, you won't be permanently damaged.

Talk to the Doctor *Lord, help me let go of anything I hold too tightly that keeps me from you.*

Happy Birthday to You!

Gary Richmond, single parents' minister at First Evangelical Free Church in Fullerton, California, and former veterinary assistant at the Los Angeles Zoo, once observed the birth of a baby giraffe. The mother giraffe was giving birth standing up, her hindquarters nearly ten feet off the ground. When the calf's front hooves and head emerged, Gary worried that the new-born would be hurt falling from such a height. He asked if someone should help the birthing of the baby giraffe, but the experienced vet warned him to stand back. He told Gary that the mother had enough strength in her legs to kick his head off, and that's exactly what she'd do if anyone approached her baby.

Minutes later the baby hurled forth, falling ten feet and landing on its back. Within seconds it rolled upright with its legs tucked under its body. The mother took a quick look, positioned herself directly over her baby, swung her leg out, and kicked her baby so hard it sent it sprawling head over heels. Gary was shocked. The baby didn't get up. Mom positioned herself over baby again and kicked it again, repeating the violent process as the baby struggled each time to rise. The mother giraffe never gave up until, amidst cheers from the zoo staff, the baby stood for the first time, wobbly and shaking, but on its own. The mother wanted the baby to learn to get up fast. In the wild it would have needed to get up as soon as possible to follow the herd and avoid being eaten alive by lions, hyenas, or leopards.

Talk to the Doctor *Lord, what do you want to teach me through the hard kicks of divorce? I want to grow stronger, run faster, and maybe learn to be smart enough to stay out of the jungle next time!*

Dead and Buried

Lazarus's already-decomposing body was in the tomb four days when Jesus, who'd been summoned earlier to come save his friend, finally showed up.

Lazarus's sister, Martha, was livid and demanded to know where Jesus had been and *why* he had let this terrible tragedy happen. She knew Jesus had the power to heal and was angry that Jesus had clearly, unquestionably—and without any apparent reason—failed her and her family.

Almost every person who has attended my divorce workshops has, at one time or another, asked God *why* he didn't change the heart of the spouse? *Why* didn't God save the marriage? How could God let this tragedy happen to the children?

The answer is in the rest of the Lazarus story.

When Lazarus was still alive but dying, and the messengers came to ask Jesus to come and heal him, Jesus already knew he was going to let his friend die. He knew he was going to use Lazarus's death to work such a fabulous miracle that faith in God would be ignited all over the countryside. Jesus knew that the terrible tragedy would be used for a greater good, for the ultimate glory of the Father.

Jesus can use your divorce to work fabulous miracles. Will you be patient and wait?

Talk to the Doctor *Father, don't let me miss the miracles you might bring from this divorce. Bring me out of the dark tomb and restore my broken spirit.*

Seeing Past Divorce

 Do you recall the story of the man born blind that Jesus healed?

"As he went along, he saw a man blind from birth. His disciples asked him, 'Rabbi, who sinned, this man or his parents, that he was born blind?'

'Neither this man nor his parents sinned,' said Jesus, 'but this happened so the work of God might be displayed in his life'" (John 9:1–3).

Jesus then spat on the ground, made some mud, put it on the man's eyes, and told him to go wash. When he did as Jesus instructed, the man was able to see. The people had wanted to know who was at fault and who was to blame for the man's blindness. Jesus tried to explain that tragedy is often permitted as a means of displaying God's glory and bringing hearts back to him.

We are often blind to the reason we were created and put upon the earth. It was not to be happy, to have a family or career, or even to have a good marriage. Each of us was specifically and intentionally created for God. Our purpose is to come to know him with our minds, love him with all our hearts, and serve him with our lives. Everything else, though worthy, is secondary—even our personal relationships and our marriages.

Whatever it takes to knock us on the head, cause us to let go, bring us out of the dark, or open our eyes, God will allow it to happen or use it to bring us to himself.

Take Your Emotional X ray *Lord, what desires have blinded me to the real reason I am here? Open my eyes to see, my mind to believe, and my heart to trust you more.*

Trust

A Perfect Parent

 Which is harder for you to do: believe in God, love God, or trust God?

After my divorce, I had to admit that I believed in God, loved him, and wanted to please him . . . but I did not completely trust him.

I recalled that when I was a little girl, my father, a developer who built residential housing subdivisions from the 1950s through the 1960s, seemed always to be at his office. When Dad came home late in the evening, he was glad to see us, would hug and kiss us all, and help us say our prayers at bedtime. He was home Sunday to cook breakfast and take us to church in the morning, read the Bible that afternoon, and carve the roast at dinner. But he was too busy to take me to the father-daughter dances, to see our school plays, or to come to the Christmas pageants. I wasn't bitter about that, because Mom always reminded us how much Dad showed he loved us by working harder than most fathers to provide for all our financial and physical needs. Despite the limited relationship, I knew Dad loved me. I always saw it in his eyes and heard it in his voice.

I trusted Dad to take care of me physically and financially, but I didn't trust that Dad would, or could, ever truly meet my emotional needs. I projected that onto my relationship with God. I knew God loved me, and I loved him, but he was busy and I would have to fend for myself.

Take Your Emotional X ray How has your relationship with your parents colored your view of God? Has lack of trust in him resulted from a lack of trust in other people?

Strong Belief, Weak Faith

Pastors and church leaders may view the following statements from pollster George Gallup, Jr. as either depressing, encouraging, or challenging:

- Americans are experiencing an intense search and hunger for the spiritual and an unprecedented desire for religious and spiritual growth.
- Many Americans seem not to know what they believe or why. And many hold traditional and nontraditional beliefs at the same time.
- Religious faith is broad but not deep, with many Americans holding strong beliefs but seeing little impact that religious faith has on individual lives and society.
- God is popular but is not first in many people's lives. "Belief in God" does not necessarily translate into "trust in God" (*Kansas City Star*, February 1, 2003).

There it is. We know he's out there but we don't trust he knows us, wants the best for us, and will show us the way. We think we have to figure it out and do it all on our own—or is it that we want to do it all on our own?

What's going on in your life that needs to be surrendered to what God wants, not what you want? What's stopping you from letting go? Is it a lack of trust?

Talk to the Doctor *Father, I admit that sometimes I do not trust you. I might trust you in some things, but not others. I might believe in my head but hold back in my heart. Will you please remind me how much you do love me and how much you promise to do for me?*

Back in the Saddle Again

After having a spouse who disappointed you, hurt, lied, or even abused you, you might find yourself with almost no trust when it comes to dating again. In my "Dear God, Send Me a Soul Mate" seminars, I advise singles who are looking for spouses to do five things when getting to know a potential new mate:

1. *Spend quality time talking and listening.* Some people share activities, but never really get to know each other. Talk, talk, talk . . . and listen.
2. *Ask the scary questions.* If you really want to know the other person, you have to be brave and bold in your questioning.
3. *Reveal your deepest desires in order to see how the person responds to you.* If you can't be safe in disclosing to someone, you will never develop trust.
4. *Investigate the person's past.* Most people are afraid to do this for fear of what they might discover. Or they just *hope* the other person is what they seem to be. Without knowing, it's hard to trust. Talk to the person's friends. Visit his or her workplace. Meet the family.
5. *Give it time.* Mutual trust takes two people, and it takes time. Stay open as time reveals deeper levels of knowing between the two of you.

Doctor's Rx To trust God, follow the same steps: Pray, then listen; be bold in your inquiries to him; reveal your heart; read Scripture to know all about God's past and how he has never let anyone down; talk to his family and friends; give trust time.

Just a Closer Walk with Thee

Educator and botanist George Washington Carver, born a slave in 1864, is noted for his scientific work with peanuts, where he developed more than three hundred products including face powder, soap, and printer's ink. He also created more than seventy-five products from pecans and more than one hundred products from sweet potatoes, including flour, shoe polish, and candy.

Scientists are trained to look for new paths that might lead to the next important discovery. They don't just trust . . . they test. Scientists rate, evaluate, calculate, and calibrate! They depend on facts, not feelings, in their experiments.

Carver had deep spiritual feelings, but he also knew the facts about God. He could measure God's love and care for his creation when he went, as he often did, outdoors to spend time in nature.

When asked for the secret behind his accomplishments, Carver said, "I have made it a rule to get up every morning at four. I go into the woods, and there I gather specimens and study the great lessons that Nature is eager to teach us. Alone in the woods each morning, I best hear and understand God's plan for me." The scientist who sought new paths consulted daily the One who could make straight his way and lead him to exciting discoveries. Carver trusted God.

Daily Dose of God's Word "Trust in the LORD with all your heart and lean not on your own understanding; in all your ways acknowledge him, and he will make your paths straight." (Prov. 3:5, 6)

Love Notes in Nature

God reveals his character to us not only through his Word but in other ways as well. George Washington Carver knew God's character through nature. Asked once to testify before a congressional committee, Carver took the ten minutes he'd been allowed, and then prepared to stop. But the committee was so fascinated by Carver that it put aside its other work and asked him to continue. So for another hour and forty-five minutes, Carver told them how you could get blue and purple pigments from Alabama red clay, how you could make fiber and rope from cornstalks, and how you could get gums, starch, and dextrin from cotton stalks. What most people saw only as disposable trash, he, with vision, saw as useful resources.

Carver likened nature to an unlimited broadcasting station through which God speaks to us every moment if we will only tune in. He said, "I never grope for methods. The method is revealed the moment I am inspired to create something new."

Divorced people often fall into the trap of trying to carefully measure their days and calculate their futures. Because of a lack of trust in God, you might be straining to create and define methods whereby you will get through recovery, attain happiness, and find what you are looking for. Is it your method . . . or his?

Physical Therapy Spend at least fifteen minutes outdoors alone, even if it's just in your backyard. Use your eyes, ears, head, and heart to tune in to what God's creation may be telling you about himself. He wants to reveal himself to you in all ways, so you will trust him.

Time

Just Do It!

Time does not heal all wounds, especially following divorce. Just as a heart patient can't expect to be cured simply by waiting a few months, a divorced person will make slow progress toward healing if he or she does nothing but wait. While time is part of the formula required for recovery, healing requires two other important components:

Work—The body works hard during healing. The patient has to cooperate by getting enough rest, taking the right medicines, and checking in with the doctor on a regular schedule. All systems in the body need to be doing repair work, creating scar tissue, or circulating antibodies. Every minute of time is well spent in every bodily system.

Outside Help—Even with a Master Physician in charge, a support team of experts can contribute to the healing process: physical therapists, X ray technicians, nurses, and laboratory workers all help. It would be foolish to not take advantage of this help, and could even lead to another heart attack or death.

After your divorce, have you been doing the work necessary to expose the wound and clean it out, or have you allowed it to fester by working, parenting, or otherwise distracting yourself? Have you enlisted the help of outside caregivers such as counselors, pastors, legal assistants, and others who can help you and your family move into emotional and spiritual health? Or are you expecting time to heal all wounds?

Today's Treatment Ask God to show you one thing you have been putting off that needs to be done for your healing. Get your calendar out, pick a date, and do it.

A Stitch in Time

Although we need to do all we can to get well, *we can't rush healing*. Ask my sister, Barb, who, after a car accident, had over one hundred stitches in her face. It happened when Barb, nineteen at the time, was missing her fiancé, Art, and decided to do something about it. A little after midnight she drove our family's car along a hypnotizing highway for several hours before she became drowsy, veered off the road, and crashed, landing upside down. Her face was cut, and her nose, hanging only by a thin piece of skin, had been nearly severed. Doctors removed pieces of shattered glass, sewed her nose back on, and held her face together with stitches.

Today Barb still has a piece of windshield glass that remained embedded in her face, just below the bridge of her nose. Because the glass was so close to her eye, the doctors were fearful about cutting deep into her skin to remove it. Instead they hoped that it would work its way out eventually like some glass shards will do. Barb's did not. At first the shard caused occasional irritation, redness, and difficulty wearing glasses, but doctors advised Barb that if the glass didn't come to the surface then her body would probably build tissue around it. Rather than getting the glass cut out, Barb chose to be patient and let time and her body help diminish the problem. Her patience paid off; she hardly notices it today.

Some struggles after divorce will take longer to heal than others, and some may be with us for years. As long as they're not making us bitter or blocking our hearts from love, we might even have to decide to just live with some things that irritate us.

Daily Dose of God's Word "We do not want you to become lazy, but to imitate those who through faith and patience inherit what has been promised." (Heb. 6:12)

Take One in the Morning

I remember when Contac time-release capsules first came out. Prior to the 1950's people had to take pills every few hours to sustain required levels of medication. Researchers began to look for chemical or mechanical methods that would gradually release drugs for a predictable therapeutic effect over an entire night or day. By 1949 they found the answer to the release-action puzzle, which was to fill capsules with pellets coated with medication that would dissolve at different times. With the new "time-release" concept, you could take one pill and it would slowly release the required dosage over an extended period of time. People were free to forget about the constant pill-popping. Because of the new technique, Contac, launched in 1960, became the world's leading cold remedy. Today, the time-release concept is widely used.

So how does this relate to healing from divorce? Some people feel they have to continually go to God and keep asking his help, as if their constant asking will insure healing. While frequent prayer is good, God's grace isn't bestowed in meagerly measured amounts. When we come to him in prayer each day and make our requests known, his help is not limited to that immediate moment. God's grace is much more like time-release capsules; throughout the day, when we need spiritual strength to handle problems, his grace is continually released whenever we need it most and without our having to worry about it.

Doctor's Rx Remember that daily time spent in prayer is like spiritual Contac, where God promises to give you what you need when you need it. Start each morning with prayer and watch what happens over time.

A Perfect Present

After divorce, time can be torture, or it can be a gift. We can spend our time waiting, worrying, and wondering . . . or we can untie the ribbons and enjoy the "present."

Shannon's heart ached when her sons began spending the night at their father's home. On the weekends the boys were with Dad, Shannon always had tons of work to do: washing, ironing, cleaning, and grocery shopping. During the week when the kids were with her, she'd make long lists of what she'd do with her free time when the boys went to Dad's. But once they walked out the door, Shannon would be so depressed she could barely get anything done. Her life then focused on Sunday night when she'd welcome the boys back, hug them tightly, and get back to normal. Shannon's excessive attachment to her sons and her fear of creating a new life for herself with new routines kept her from moving more quickly toward healing. One day she had coffee with some other divorced parents, including Mike, who knew just what Shannon was going through.

He told her, "Shannon, your boys are safe and having fun at their dad's, right? Well, you're safe too, and God wants *you* to have some fun!" Mike added, "We divorced parents have a gift married parents almost never get—long weekends all to ourselves, to do whatever we want!"

That was just what Shannon needed to hear. Last time I heard from her, she had taken up golf and was reading more of her favorite books.

Band-Aid for Your Soul Give yourself a gift: Plan something fabulous for the next weekend you are alone. If your kids are adults and gone, do something fun anyway!

Your Ex-Spouse

Who's to Blame?

After the divorce, Jack lamented, "Linda and I had agreed on custody and visitation issues, but her mother decided Linda wasn't getting enough time with the children. It was like that in our marriage. Whenever her mother stuck her nose into our business, Linda had trouble standing up for me or alongside me in our decisions. I felt violated, cheated on, and abandoned. I guess Linda will never change."

You might be having difficulty with your ex-spouse over family or financial issues. It's tempting, and may seem safer, to blame a third party for making issues difficult to resolve—your accountant, attorney, other family members, or the new spouse. Because you once loved and became one flesh with your ex-spouse, you may feel a lingering bond with him or her that will naturally pull you to want some measure of peace and harmony even in your divorced relationship. When you get tired of being angry with your ex, you'll seek someone else to blame for lingering difficulties.

If you both get along together one-on-one, but one of you acts badly when parents, lawyers, or a new spouse is present, don't be quick to let your former spouse off the hook and blame the third parties. *No person is so weak that he or she is forced to be difficult with you by some powerful third person.* It's more likely your ex-spouse is freely choosing his or her response to you to avoid rejection and keep the peace. Triangulating (using or blaming a third person) reflects our own insecurity and fear of losing what we see as the power position.

Talk to the Doctor *Lord, help me see things clearly, and to address the real problems with love and forgiveness.*

It's Never the Same

Frank had always been sexually attracted to his wife. "Even when things got really bad, our sex life was still always good. It was the glue that held us together for as long as our marriage lasted."

Maria always felt better when after an argument she and her husband, Tony, made love. "We could put aside all our anger or hurt and come together in love. It was good. I really miss that part of our life."

One of the common temptations divorced people have, especially if there's no intense anger or resentment between them, is to end up in bed again together. "Sex with the ex" is reported to be common in as many as 45 percent of divorce situations. While some will be aghast at such a thought, others see it as normal and natural, especially if that was the least troubled part of the marriage.

Kathy told me, "I really wanted to reconcile, but Tony didn't. I knew that. He felt guilty for leaving me and had been coming over more and more to see the kids, and staying later and later. I hoped after we made love he would change his mind. He didn't. The hurt in my heart is even worse than it was before."

Have you had your heart broken again by your ex after divorce? Don't try to use sex outside marriage to feel better. It will ultimately undo healing and lay open a fresh heart wound.

Sex is beautiful with lifelong commitment. Without it, it hurts.

Talk to the Doctor *Father, with all my soul, with my entire body, I ache to hold and be held again. Let me feel your arms around me so that I don't put others or myself into temptation.*

When Looking Good Is Bad

My friend had cosmetic surgery and was given strict instructions not to engage in any sports or go into the sun for at least six weeks. She felt great, though, and decided that fresh sunshine and some activity would be healthy. She was anxious to go out in public looking good, so she did. After a weekend of waterskiing at the river, she regretted her actions. She had a good time and felt fabulous, but permanently damaged her skin and undid some of the surgery.

It might be good that you and your ex-spouse get along and even socialize, but maybe not. It feels good, you look good, but what damage are you doing to others, especially your children, by what seems to be a good thing? Divorced couples that cohost birthday parties and share holiday meals together tend to gauge their "recovery" on how social they can still be with each other. Being able to say, "Look, everyone, we get along great!" sometimes helps to heal the guilt, regret, or fear of accusations. But even though things look good on the surface, they can be doing damage to underlying emotional layers. If you are friendly with an ex, watch for these potential problems:

- Getting along on the surface but denying emotional wounds develops a false persona, ignores the truth, and internally traps infected emotions. In short, it's living a lie. You can be kind without being cozy.
- Genuine caring is ideal, but continuing to function as a family might give either person, or almost always the children, false hopes of reconciliation.

Take Your Emotional X ray *Lord, show me where my good intentions might actually be hurting someone. Please bring balance into the way I interact with my ex-spouse.*

New Thoughts for Old Loves

While some get along just fine, most divorced people have strained relations with an ex-husband or ex-wife. After all, you didn't get along well enough to make the marriage work. Expect trouble, but be thankful when things go smoothly. If they don't, give careful thought to redefining the relationship: be honest, be real, be loving, and be smart.

Rethink Your Expectations: Realistic expectations will help minimize your anger. Do you still need to grieve?

Keep Contact Short: If you frequently argue, limit phone calls, emails, and time spent together, and keep topics of conversation focused on the kids.

Don't Push Parenting on Your Ex: If your ex-spouse has different morals or lacks parenting skills, don't try to co-parent. Do your best and trust God to get the kids through these years.

Don't Be Angry for Everyone: Don't do your children's anger work for them or try to fix their relationship with the other parent. Teach them to accept reality, grieve, and maintain a loving attitude.

Protect Yourself and Your Family: Learn smart and loving communication skills. Overcome fears of saying yes or no.

Daily Dose of God's Word: "The wisdom of the prudent is to give thought to their ways, but the folly of fools is deception." (Prov. 14:8)

Move Over, Darling

How much room do you have in your heart?

Marilyn was divorced and had been remarried a little over a year. Her daughter, Kim, had just graduated from high school and was planning to go to college. Marilyn's ex-husband had set up a trust fund for both Kim and her brother for college tuition and related expenses, and Kim was depending on the money for school.

Shortly after graduation, Kim called her dad to ask for the money. Her father insisted he had already given Kim the money and that there was none left. Kim was shocked! When she hung up, she told her mother and stepdad what her father had said.

Marilyn was appalled. She was furious that her ex-spouse not only lied to their daughter, but obviously had no intention of helping her get a higher education. As she stood there in frustration and disbelief, Marilyn said, "I hate him, I hate him!"

Her wise husband replied, "Honey, please don't hate him."

"Why not? What's it to you if I hate him?" Marilyn shot back.

Her husband came over and put his arms around her, pulling her to him. "Because if you have hate in your heart for him, you have that much less room in your heart for *me!*"

Marilyn listened and made room in her heart again for love. Have you done the same?

Talk to the Doctor *Lord, please help me remember that you want me to keep a standing reservation in my heart for love.*

Reconciliation

Divorce: the New Reality Show

It took some time, but after his heart surgery, my father reconciled himself to the fact he could never smoke his favorite cigars again. He faced the reality that his heart was prone to attack and he'd never be able to do some of the things he would have liked to do.

We more often think of reconciliation especially after divorce, as getting back together with an ex-spouse; and if there's any chance of such reconciliation, pursue it, especially if you have children. A word of caution: If there was any kind of abuse, or long-standing patterns of selfishness, dishonesty, or other spiritual and emotional "diseases" that could set you and your family up for future heart attacks, you might not want to reconcile yourselves to the old way things were in the marriage. Rather than reconcile, you can rebuild. Regardless of your approach, reconciliation or rebuilding takes two and it takes time.

Sometimes, for whatever reason, you cannot be reconciled within marriage, but you can be reconciled to the person. You can change your attitude toward him or her by getting rid of fears that bind you. You can get rid of hate and hurt. You can choose to be kind, fair, and courteous at whatever level of contact you have.

If you never see the person again, or if he or she harbors anger or is a threat to you or your family, and you can't be reconciled to the person, you can be reconciled to reality. This can be a healing type of reconciliation—an honest acceptance of the situation without always wishing it was different.

Talk to the Doctor *Dear God, please help me see and accept the realities of life.*

Cleaning Up Your Act

George Bernard Shaw, the brilliant playwright whose play *Pygmalion* became the Oscar-winning movie *My Fair Lady,* once said, "The worst sin towards our fellow creatures is not to hate them, but to be indifferent to them: that's the essence of inhumanity."

Do you remember in the movie how Professor Henry Higgins casually overlooked grimy flower girl, Eliza Doolittle, outside the London theatre? He didn't hate her; he was indifferent to her—so emotionally removed and intellectually detached that he couldn't care less if she lived or died. When he carried that attitude into their later relationship, it infuriated her!

Sometimes after divorce, if we've expended lots of angry energy toward an ex-spouse, we pull back to the other extreme. We convince ourselves we couldn't care less if they live or die. We move on. It's over and done with. Our angry feelings are gone, and we assume a rather cool (maybe condescending) consideration of them as part of our past. In the same way that hurt or anger blocked our hearts from receiving the fullness of God's love, so too will casual indifference block our soul's arteries.

Instead of becoming indifferent to an ex-spouse in order to protect yourself from pain, you are called to reconcile. That means coming to a place where you can again offer him or her genuine caring, well-wishing, and prayers. You don't have to fix, see, or even speak with an ex-spouse, but you do have to hold him or her somewhere in your heart.

Take Your Emotional Temperature What is keeping you from genuinely caring about someone who has hurt you deeply?

It Takes Two, and It Takes Time

When I was a younger, single, workingwoman, with no husband in sight, I decided to adopt a little girl. I figured since I had a home and natural mothering skills, I should share my blessings with a less-fortunate child. The county adoption agency brought me Ricki when she was eight years old.

For several years I tried desperately to make a good home for my new daughter. Unfortunately, Ricki, having been raised in the streets, was severely neglected and abused in every way. The psychiatrist who helped me with her revealed that older adoptive children are almost always abused and troubled. If the county had revealed that, it was unlikely anyone would have taken her. I felt cheated and betrayed. It was one of the most difficult periods of my life.

When she began to act out in ways that threatened our family and friends, I knew I could no longer handle her and had to send her back to the county agency, where she grew up in a group home until she was eighteen. It broke my heart, and I felt like a failure for a long time afterward. Even though I eventually reconciled myself to the reality of the situation, I longed to be reconciled to her. But knowing that adoption whereabouts are kept secret, I thought I would never see her again.

Years later I got a phone call. It was Ricki. We met for lunch where I listened to her story and got to tell her everything I had wanted to say. She did not ask me to, nor did I want to, get involved in her life again, but that day we were reconciled. It was a gift to both of us.

Doctors Rx Ask God for the chance to reconcile with someone you once loved. Then be patient and wait for that person to come around, even if it takes years. You won't regret it.

The Kids

Lord, You're a Lifesaver!

Have you ever taught a child to swim? My stepson, Mikey, was four when I took him to the swimming pool. He clamped his arms around my neck, his little legs squeezed tightly around my waist, and I thought I'd have to get a tire iron to pry him off. It was time to overcome his fear of the water, so I firmly peeled him off and gently pushed him away, still holding him with one hand. When I finally let go of his hand for just a second, he panicked, splashed furiously, and grabbed on to the kid next to him, pulling him down below the surface. I rescued them before they both drowned.

When we divorce, we often go into a similar panic. The fingers that intertwined with ours as we walked back down the church aisle have let go. We might not recognize it as panic, but much like Mikey, believing we can't keep our heads above water, we reach out and grab the nearest loving hands around: an older parent's, a good friend's, or our kids'.

Although their unconditional love and comfort ease the pain, kids are not meant to be our lifesavers after divorce. They are emotionally thrashing around too, and if we hang on to them too tightly, relying on them to fill our emotional needs for companionship, comfort, or counsel, we'll pull them down with us.

Reach out first for God, and let him lead you to appropriate hands to hold.

Daily Dose of God's Word "The disciples went and woke him, saying, 'Lord, save us! We're going to drown!' He replied, 'You of little faith, why are you so afraid?' Then he got up and rebuked the winds and the waves, and it was completely calm.'" (Matt. 8:25, 26)

Those Kids Are Mine!

"But Mom, it's not fair!" I whined. I was ten years old, and Mom had just taken away my doll. Well, it wasn't really my doll. My two sisters and I had each received the same doll but with different colored hair for Christmas. Serena had left her doll out in the rain, and I'd rescued it. I shampooed her yarn hair, fluffed her dress, and lined her up on my bed with the rest of my "babies."

For months I kept Serena's doll until one day she came into my bedroom and announced, "That's MY doll and I want it." My motherly instinct leapt out like a lion's. "No way! You don't deserve to have this doll because I'm the one who cleaned her, cared for her, and loved her more than you. I deserve to have this doll. You don't. You just left her out in the yard! Get out of my room!"

Serena ran out crying loudly, "MOM!"

After pro and con arguments, Mom gave the doll back to Serena and reminded me, "Just because you take good care of something and love it doesn't make it belong to you."

I learned then what all parents going through divorce should understand: When our kids are taken away through a custody agreement or even just for a weekend with their other parent, it's normal to feel pain and loss. Remember though, our children are not really our own; they're God's. Our job is to love them, let others love them, and get them ready to be sent off.

Talk to the Doctor *Father, I know life will reclaim my children and that I am only a temporary guardian. You are their real parent. Help me to release my children however and whenever it happens, trusting that you will continue to watch over them.*

105

Spelling Lessons

When there's a vacuum in the family created by Mom or Dad's absence, parents mistakenly put their children into one or more of these four unhealthy roles:

Adult—A divorced mom "adultifies" her son when she tells him he must now be the "little man" of the house, and a divorced dad does the same when he tells his daughter he'll need to lean on her now that Mom's not there. Casting children into adult rolls forces them to assume responsibilities God never intended them to have and may warp their future relationships.

Baby—The other extreme is babying our kids out of pity for their pain, or to make them happy. Indulgent parenting is a form of narcissism: We do it because we really want someone to baby us! It's okay to go easy on them for a while, but then get back on track so they can keep growing.

Companion—Don't rob their childhood by making your children your best friends or surrogate spouse.

Deity—When we place our kids above everything else, we might be making little gods out of them. There's a difference between a healthy prioritizing of children's needs and putting them first in all situations. Making kids the center of the universe hurts them. God and those he put in authority (parents) should run the home. Who's the head of *your* family?

Talk to the Doctor *Lord, it may be elementary, but I sometimes have emotional dyslexia with the ABCs of divorce. Please help me keep my family priorities in the right order.*

Unexpected Joys

Good things can sometimes come out of divorce.

Patti is a firm believer in the blessings that God can bring if we stay close to him through anything. She told me, "One of the gifts that came through my divorce, and there were many, was the development of a much closer relationship with one of my twin daughters, Jamie. She was our quiet child, undemanding, and seldom the center of attention in our busy family of six.

"When our marriage ended, for a period of time it was just Jamie and me. She was eighteen. We cooked together, snuggled on the couch, shopped, and shared our hearts' desires. I'm quite sure that if my marriage had remained intact, Jamie and I would never have formed the precious bond that came as a result of our time together. God revealed his love for me through my daughter, and her sweet presence was a balm during the healing time.

"Thankfully, I had the chance to give Jamie what she never demanded but always longed for, a parent's undivided attention. So my advice—as hard as it may be—is to look for the blessings God is bestowing on you during this most painful of times."

As Patti experienced, even our adult children can be continued sources of love and comfort. Maybe you don't have children, or yours have been taken away or turned against you. Ask God to send you other "children" to love.

Daily Dose of God's Word "And we know that in all things God works for the good of those who love him, who have been called according to his purpose." (Rom. 8:28)

The Other Woman

And God Fashioned Woman

The wedding day was fast approaching and nothing could dampen Jennifer's excitement, not even her parents' recent nasty divorce. Her mother finally found the perfect dress for the event and would be the best-dressed Mother of the Bride ever!

A week later, Jennifer was horrified to discover her new, young stepmother, Barbie, had purchased the same dress. She asked Barbie to exchange the dress, but Barbie refused, exclaiming, "Absolutely not! I'm going to wear this dress. I look like a million in it!" Jennifer told her mother, who graciously replied, "Never mind dear, I'll get another dress. After all, it's your day, not ours." Two weeks later, Jennifer and her mother went shopping and found another dress. At lunch, Jennifer asked, "Mom, what are you going to do with the first dress? It was so expensive, and you really don't have anywhere else to wear it."

"Of course I do," the mother replied. "I'm wearing it to the rehearsal dinner."

I laughed when I read this story, having been both a first wife and a second wife. The tension between two competitive women can always be broken when one of them surrenders her desires for being the best or being in control. God wants us to be free of fear, to be loving, forgiving, and trusting in him. That's what will make us look—and feel—like a million.

Daily Dose of God's Word "Your beauty should not come from outward adornment, such as braided hair and the wearing of gold jewelry and fine clothes. Instead, it should be that of your inner self, the unfading beauty of a gentle and quiet spirit, which is of great worth in God's sight." (1 Pet. 3:3, 4)

The Bitterness of Betrayal

An arrow piercing your heart—that's what it feels like when your spouse has an emotional or sexual affair. Your own failed marriage may not have included infidelity with another person, but there was "the other woman" nonetheless. When any outside force draws your spouse's heart away from you and is given the time, attention, and priority that rightfully belong to you, there has been a form of infidelity.

What drew you and your spouse apart? It may have masked as work, money, or the kids, but it was probably selfishness, pride, or unforgiveness. Whatever it was, it lured you or your ex-spouse and held on tightly, not against your will but with deliberate participation. That's what hurts.

Marital love is both a pale imitation and a beautiful model of the deep and everlasting love God has for us. He provides for our needs, loves us totally, and brings us great joy. In return he desires our firstfruits of time, attention, and priority. In the Old Testament, God declares Israel an adulterous spouse for having forsaken his love. You may not have been unfaithful to your spouse, but have you been unfaithful to God? Even in little ways, have you spent too much time with or pursued things that keep you from him?

The next time you find yourself condemning an unfaithful spouse or "the other woman," stop and remember that, in a way, you're no better than he or she is. We're all sinners. But we can all be forgiven and all are deeply loved.

Daily Dose of God's Word "For all have sinned and fall short of the glory of God." (Rom. 3:23)

Loving God, Hating Others?

Barbara was devastated. Her husband had a long-term affair, divorced her, and married the other woman. As time passed, Barbara watched her children become attached to their new stepmom and new little half brother, Joey, but for years Barbara could barely stand the thought of either of them. About ten years after the divorce, Barbara's ex-husband dropped dead of a heart attack. Barbara was shocked and flooded with old emotions when she heard the news. She attended the funeral for her children's sake, but refused to look at or speak to her children's stepmother and half brother. Barbara's daughter Marsha finally confronted her.

"I know you were deeply hurt by the divorce, Mom, but the way you've treated Cindy and Joey for years is rotten. No matter what they did wrong, Cindy has loved us, and Joey is our brother. We love them. God loves them. You hate them." Marsha left her mother to think about what she'd said.

When you find yourself bitter toward the other woman, or the third party with whom your ex-spouse has been unfaithful or has married, know that God wants you to change two things: your attitude and your actions.

You don't have to like the third party, become his or her best friend, or invite the person over to your home. You don't have to accept what the other party did as right or pretend it didn't hurt. But you do have to let God take care of him or her and see that person as he does: weak, like you, but deeply loved.

Take Your Emotional Temperature *Lord, show me how I can change my attitude. Let me see other people through your eyes.*

Small Note, Big Woman

The story of Barbara and her daughter Marsha is true. After Barbara decided to change her attitude, she responded to God's urgings to change her actions, too. On a Saturday morning she sat down and wrote to the other woman:

Dear Cindy:

I know you and I have never spoken, and this is the hardest letter I've ever had to write. My children have told me that you have always been a wonderful stepmother to them . . . I understand when Dick died he left you with no insurance and no source of income to cover living expenses.

Dick and I had an old insurance policy that will keep me comfortable for the rest of my life. This letter is to inform you that I have instructed my attorney to deposit a regular income for you and Joey into your bank account each month until Joey is eighteen. My attorney will be contacting you. I would prefer it if you would please not call or contact me. This is very difficult for me and I don't know if I will ever be able to be your friend. But my children love you. Because you have taken care of my children's needs while they were with you these last ten years, I want to help you take care of your son.

Sincerely, Barbara

Take Your Emotional X ray Is there a letter or phone call inside you that should be written or made? What's blocking your heart from changing your attitude and actions?

The New Stepparent

More Love for Your Kids

Do you struggle with your relationship with your children's new stepparent? Some of us get along well with our ex-spouse's new mate, but most of us don't. Even if your children don't have a new stepparent, they *will* have other new people come into their lives as a result of the divorce: possibly people of whom you do not approve or who are bad influences on them. Maybe, though, the new people will bring something beautiful you never dreamed of into your children's lives.

My stepson, Mikey, wasn't connected to me with an umbilical cord, but the love that grew between us tied our souls together. That little face and impish smile struck my heart the day I met him. As his stepmom, I was able to help him learn multiplication tables, how to bake chocolate cookies, and how to say the Lord's Prayer. While his mother put her heart and energies into his school and sports, I got to contribute arts, music, and piano lessons. Sometimes she didn't like what I did, and sometimes I didn't like what she did. But we both loved him and gave him the best of what we each had.

Today little Mikey is Mike, a teenager who has some scars as a result of his parents' divorce, but also extra love, encouragement, and support from all the adults in his life who care: parents, stepparents, teachers, neighbors, and pastors . . . and me! God loves your kids more than you do and will help you parent them by bringing others to do his work in their hearts. Will you trust him with their lives?

Take Your Emotional Temperature Is my heart closed by fear or jealousy toward the new stepparent, or open to God's leading?

Not Always a Fairy Tale

Cinderella's stepmother should have been turned into child protective services for her verbal and physical abuse of the orphaned girl. For that matter, those ugly stepsisters should've been turned in too! Alas, in fairy tale times there were no social agencies to help protect children from abusive adults. Today, however, there are.

You may be faced with some genuine concern about the interaction of the new stepparent and your children, especially with the rapidly rising rates today of immoral behavior, lack of healthy boundaries, casual sex, and drug use in American homes, and even physical and sexual abuse. The wicked stepparent gets that reputation for a very real reason: A large majority of cases of sexual abuse of children involves a stepparent, the new boyfriend, or a girlfriend. When there are no blood ties, sick adults feel freer to cross boundaries.

What are your choices? If you have concerns, you can let them eat you up and hold you hostage to your fears and bitterness, or you can do something about them. Be rigorously honest about your motives. Ask God to reveal the truth to your heart. Beg for his grace to have the courage to speak up and take legal action against what you suspect, or the courage to let go and relax. Get as much information as you can, seek counseling, and spend much time in prayer.

Talk to the Doctor *Lord, I just want my kids to have a "happily ever after." Show me if these fears are just my own ego trying to make the other parent(s) look bad or if I need to take action. Please give me a quiet spirit and a calm assurance in you.*

Making God Proud of You

Do you want to make brownie points with your children? Give them permission to love their new stepparent.

Kristi's daughter, Melanie, always came home from weekends at her dad's with stories about Susan.

"Watch, Mom. Susan showed me how to make a snowflake with scissors and paper!"

"Daddy and Susan took me to the movies, and Susan and I split a giant popcorn!"

"Susan bought me this new dress, Mom!"

It may kill you to hear all this because Susan was the one with whom your husband had an affair right before you divorced. You don't have to like Susan, be her friend, or spend any time with her. But let your child love her and receive love from her.

Can you move past the jealous feeling that someone else is competing for your child's love? Can you let go of the fear that you can't control every aspect of your child's life? Can you come to a place of forgiveness and peace? Our children sense when we disapprove of or resent another person, and they'll either withhold love, refuse to receive it, learn to lie, or hide it from you. *If you free your own heart, you free your child's heart as well.*

Doctor's Rx   Find out the new stepparent's birthday and mark it on your calendar. Help your child pick a card and small gift each year for him or her.

Friends

Blessings in the Blizzards

Freddi Dogterom, an author and speaker in Canada's Arctic, and a dear friend of mine, told me a fascinating story of "Inukshuks:"

"The Arctic is a breathtakingly beautiful but potentially dangerous place to live. Of all the dangers, including wild beasts, the most feared is probably getting lost out on the tundra. A person could wander for days until a predator or exhaustion killed him. In the Arctic, above the tree line, the land is flat with no trees or landmarks to mark the way. Forget a compass; the magnetic North Pole makes it useless. Since the population is sparse and the terrain inaccessible, there are no roads, and therefore no road maps." Freddi added, "There's no AAA in the Arctic, Rose. It's very easy to get lost."

Freddi continued, "An Inukshuk (in-OOK-shook) is a pile of stones made to resemble a human form. The Intuit natives would build these stone figures to help others find their way. Sighting an Inukshuk was a great source of comfort. Because they resemble people, they are called 'Living Stones.' In the Intuit language, Inukshuk means 'Stone Man Who Points the Way.'"

I thought immediately of the empty, barren landscape after divorce, where we all can get lost. God often points the way for us through a trusted friend—a strong and steady Inukshuk he built just for us.

Daily Dose of God's Word "I guide you in the way of wisdom and lead you along straight paths." (Prov. 4:11)

Help in Rocky Times

While Freddi lived in Canada's Arctic region, an old Intuit woman, Ida Aleekuk, taught her how to sew leather and fur and to bead *mukluks*—high boots made from the skin and fur of a moose, caribou, or seal. Ida also taught her how to build an Inukshuk.

"Each stone is carefully selected and placed in a particular order," Ida told Freddi. "Don't just go for the pretty ones. You need strong ones that will fit and give support. The headstone is the most important one of all. It defines the character of your Inukshuk." Freddi spent many hours with Ida and made hundreds of Inukshuks.

"Each figure was unique, each one special in its own way," said Freddi. "Soon they were not just a pile of stones to me. Surprisingly my Inukshucks became like real people. Some were big, some little, some sturdy, and some weak. I made plain ones and pretty ones, but each was special."

Years later when Freddi moved, Ida gave her advice about friends. "Build a new Inukshuk, but build it with new friends. Just like picking the rocks, pick each one with care. They will be your living stones. Pick some for strength, some for support, and some to fill in gaps in your life. Your new Inukshuk will help point the way."

Physical Therapy Make a list of your closest friends or supporters during the time after your divorce. Go outside and pick a special rock for each, saving the headstone for your most special friend. Then with some glue you get at a craft store, make an Inukshuk to remind you of the gift God gives you of friends who point the way.

Tough Love, True Love

Whatever you do, don't let your friends help you bash your ex-spouse.

When I got divorced, one of my girlfriends told me, "I never liked him from the beginning. You always deserved better." That made me feel supported, but inside I was slightly wounded because part of me still loved my ex-husband and always would. The same friend called me every few months afterward to tell me negative gossip about my ex-husband. "I heard he's . . ." You know the type of comment I mean.

Another girlfriend, though, just looked sad when she learned of the pain both of us had gone through. She listened attentively when I poured out my heart, but never said a bad word about anyone. Amazingly she was able to show sympathy and compassion for both of us without excusing either of us. I was acutely aware of what she did *not* say about my ex-husband, and I respected her for it. As time went by, she, too, ran into my ex-husband in our small town. She told me about it without commenting or judging him. That's the kind of friend I want and the kind I want to be.

True friends are those who will hold you accountable to a higher standard, not just make you feel better. They'll encourage you, but admonish you when they see you becoming bitter or vengeful. If you are making a fool of yourself, they'll tell you, but love you anyway. They don't necessarily take your side; they take God's side. They point the way.

Daily Dose of God's Word "Wounds from a friend can be trusted, but an enemy multiplies kisses." (Prov. 27:6)

Where to Get Help

Christic in the Community

Jesus' friend Lazarus was buried in the customary manner in those days: wrapped head-to-toe in burial linens, much like mummies were wrapped in ancient Egypt. It must have taken hours to carefully wrap the body, and even more hours to carefully unwrap Lazarus after Jesus raised him from the dead.

Until I read this oft-overlooked verse one day in the New Testament story of Lazarus, I never realized how fully God uses the Christian community to be his arms and legs, his heart and hands. The words Jesus spoke as specific instruction to the community, the family and the friends—untie Lazarus—reminded me we truly are the body of Christ:

"The dead man came out, his hands and feet wrapped with strips of linen, and a cloth around his face. Jesus said to them, 'Take off the grave clothes and let him go.'" (John 11:44).

Jesus invoked the Father's power and made the miracle happen, but he didn't stick around and untie Lazarus himself. He assigned that job to the people. Our Lord does the same today. He can heal a broken heart, but he appoints those around us to unwrap us from mental, emotional, spiritual, physical, financial, or sexual ties that bind us. If we want full healing, we need to seek out and allow God's people to participate with him in our recovery.

Take Your Emotional X ray What fear is blocking your mind or heart from seeking professional Christian counseling? Jesus expects you to let others help untie you.

Help Me? Fat Chance!

One day an overweight woman complaining of severe chest pains called 911. A few minutes later, the fire engine arrived. Heading up the response team was a young, attractive, female paramedic.

The woman eyed the girl intently. "You're the assistant. You're not one of the qualified medical people, right?" the woman asked. The young paramedic was wearing a pink lab coat with matching pink ribbon in her ponytail, and had a bright blue stethoscope around her neck. She did not fit the typical image of a seasoned medical specialist.

"No," smiled the girl, "I *am* the paramedic. I know I look young, and I . . ."

The woman cut her off. "I think I have a rather serious problem here, young lady, and I need to see someone with experience. Can you please get one of your supervisors?"

For a moment the surprised young woman just stared and then began to tell the woman that she was trained to help her. The woman, now sweating profusely, refused any treatment. "I want someone older and more qualified." The paramedic tried to explain calmly that they had just come from visiting kindergartners and that her uniform was not standard, but the woman could not hear her. She'd just lapsed into a coma, suffered a massive heart attack, and could not be revived.

Take Your Emotional Pulse Sometimes help comes in a form we do not expect. Have you refused to seek help from someone that God has sent after your divorce because the person did not fit your preconceived description of being qualified?

Get on Your Knees and Bray

Balaam had been given strict instructions by God to do only what God commanded him. One morning he arose, saddled up his donkey, and rode off on a mission without waiting for God to tell him where to go or what to do. God was angry with Balaam.

To divert Balaam from his plans, God sent a mighty angel to stand in the road. Balaam didn't see the angel, but his donkey did; so the donkey veered off into the field. Balaam beat her to get her back on the road. Two more times the donkey saw the angel and tried to change course, but Balaam, still blind to what God was trying to tell him, beat her each time. Obviously the angel was not enough, so God allowed the donkey to open her mouth and speak audibly to her master, begging him to consider how she had always been faithful and would never steer her master wrong. When a shocked Balaam stopped to think about it, he realized she must be right. Suddenly he saw the angel standing before him with drawn sword, and he dropped in terror to his knees. God had his attention now, and Balaam finally changed course.

You may have plans on how to recover after divorce: bypassing the pain, withdrawing into depression, fighting fiercely in court, seeking a new relationship, or pursuing some other path that is not what God intends. Someone close to you in your life probably sees what direction you need to go and is trying to tell you. Is it a friend, a counselor, or your pastor?

Maybe you should be more like Balaam's donkey. Stop and listen, or God may have to put a sword in your path.

Talk to the Doctor *Lord, open my eyes and show me the right way to go.*

124

Winners Weigh in Weekly

Years ago I went to Weight Watchers and learned a lot about nutrition. I also learned what eating habits I had that needed to change so I would not turn into two-ton Tessie. Success required three things: the will to change, self-discipline, and someone to teach me new habits. I'm thankful that what I learned has helped me keep excess weight off for over twenty-five years. I'm fit, healthy, and happy, and I can still enjoy a buttery bearclaw danish now and then for breakfast.

One of the most common complaints I hear from people who attend my divorce recovery seminars is that their individual counseling or marriage counseling didn't work. People say that about Weight Watchers, too. But I know the reason self-improvement programs and counseling don't always work is that people don't follow the program. They only do part of it, they don't stick with it long enough, they "fudge," or they give up when it gets too difficult.

Experienced counselors, teachers, authors, therapists, pastors, or others can be the people God uses to help you through divorce. He promises to instruct us, but as he has done for thousands of years, he is apt to use human beings to bring us the help we need. I needed help, education, and encouragement when it came to my eating habits. I couldn't do it alone. When I was prideful or lazy and insisted on doing it on my own, I failed. When I let others teach me, I succeeded. What is stopping you from being open to outside help in your divorce recovery?

Daily Dose of God's Word "I will instruct you and teach you in the way you should go; I will counsel you and watch over you." (Ps. 32:8)

Money

Wealthy and Wise

 A man was diagnosed as being terminally ill. "How much time do I have, Doctor?" the man asked his physician.

The answer came, "A year, maybe two."

For a while the man lived much the same as he had in the past, but then something moved in his heart. "What am I doing still working? Why am I putting money in my savings account?" he asked himself. For the next eighteen months he began to live the way his heart told him; he gave generously, he lived as if each day were his last, and he loved with no agenda or fear of the future.

On his deathbed he confided to his pastor, "The last eighteen months have been the richest of my life."

You've heard the old saying, "You can't take it with you." We all believe it's true, but how many of us live our lives according to that belief? If you're young or have the responsibility of a family, you have to be concerned about financial security for today and the future. But you might be forgetting that true wealth of the heart comes from generosity of the spirit.

What if you have little or no money to spend on yourself or on others? The desire for it, the "need" for it, or the fear of not having it in the future can still enslave you.

How has money got a hold on your heart? Has fear of the future got you in its grip?

Daily Dose of God's Word "Consider how the lilies grow. They do not labor or spin. Yet I tell you, not even Solomon in all his splendor was dressed like one of these" (Luke 12:27).

You'll Leave for Home Without It

A stingy, old family-law attorney who had been diagnosed with a terminal illness was determined to prove wrong the saying, "You can't take it with you."

After much thought and consideration, the man finally figured out how to take at least some of his money with him when he died. He instructed his wife to go to the bank and withdraw enough money to fill two pillowcases. He then directed her to take the bags of money to the attic and put them directly above where his bed was in the bedroom. His plan: When he passed away, he would reach out and grab the bags as he floated on up to heaven.

Several weeks after the funeral as the deceased lawyer's wife was cleaning the attic, she came upon the two pillowcases stuffed with cash.

"Oh, that darned old fool," she exclaimed. "I knew he should have had me put the money down in the basement."

A cute twist on an old saying, but a reminder nonetheless that our eyes should be on our final destination more than on the money we have or don't have. During divorce, or afterward when the courts have finalized what allowances you'll get, you can lose sight of the big picture. Jesus lovingly reminds us over and over that riches that endure are those stored in heaven.

Today's Treatment Your financial life after divorce may be a temporary hell, but focus just for today on the riches of eternal life in heaven.

Rich Man, Poor Man

One day a rich father took his son to the country with the firm purpose of showing him how poor people have to live. They spent a day and a night at the farm of an impoverished family. When they got back from the trip, the father asked his son if he'd learned anything about being poor.

The son answered, "I saw that we have a dog at home, and they have four. We have a pool that reaches to the middle of the garden; they have a creek that has no end. We have imported lanterns in our yard, but they have the stars. Our patio reaches to the property line, but they have the whole horizon."

When the boy finished, the father stood speechless. His son added, "Thanks, Dad, for showing me how poor we are!"

Money is never the problem. It's our attitude toward money that's the problem. Arguments over finances and property can continue for years after a divorce, focused on three main areas of concern: child support, spousal support, and division of property. The real problem is the fear of not being able to provide for ourselves and our children, which translates to lack of faith that God will take care of us. We compound the issues with our need for control, selfishness, and even revenge.

Is there anything blocking your heart from a healthy attitude about money?

Talk to the Doctor *Lord, I get so scared of being financially insecure. I give you control of my heart so money, or the fear of not having it, doesn't control me.*

Taking Charge of the Charge Cards

Every child should have a roof over his head, clothes on his back, a meal in his belly, and someone to love. Anything beyond that is extra.

Despite what we as parents have come to expect or hope for ourselves and our children financially, life doesn't come with any guarantees. Moreover, we need to get over the idea that our children "deserve better." Little Johnny and Jessica don't need another video game or the latest sugarcoated cereal at five bucks a box. They need priceless love and guidance into adulthood.

The failure of many divorced parents to accept this reality, grieve the "loss," and put their faith back in God keeps them in angry bondage to financial bitterness. Instead of being bitter about your lack of money, try putting some sweetness on the cereal of your life by:

Living within your means: Free yourself of the tyranny and stress of always wanting more. Constant anger at your financial situation will drain you of joy, incline you to gain weight, send you into depression, set you up for heart attacks and cancer, or worse . . . put new wrinkles on your face!

Staying on a budget: Believe it or not, budgets help you get more of what you want! Teach the kids how to work a budget. It will become a valuable lifelong habit.

Putting the kids to work: Nothing builds kids' self-esteem like helping around the house. Let the kids work for what they want. Prepare them for life and give them a gift they can bring to their future spouses: a willingness to work hard.

Today's Treatment Next Saturday make homemade pizza and a new budget.

The Courts

Self-Restraining Orders

Someone once said, "Death is cheaper than divorce because a pine box costs only a fraction of the attorney's fee." He was right.

Getting trapped in drawn out court battles over your house, money, or the kids constitutes a lingering death with a high price. The court system is complicated, confusing, and commonly crooked! Many guides and workbooks can help you understand court proceedings and guide you through the legal maze, but very few will tell you the emotional and spiritual price you can expect to pay: ongoing anger, bitterness, and worry; drained energy, emptied savings account, passing the anger on to your kids and friends, being continually obsessed with winning, and often refusing to trust in God to take care of you and your children in the future.

Like lots of divorced people, I've been in and out of courts so many times over custody, visitation, and support issues it would make your head spin. I'd always hoped in the idealism of our country's principles of justice and the protection of the family. Sometimes it works, most of the time it does not. Even if the cause for which you fight is justified, you are always at the whim of an imperfect legal system, an uninformed or biased judge, and the prejudices of our society as a whole. The bottom line—avoid the courts at all costs if you can.

To the extent you can work things out with an ex-spouse, do so, even if you don't get everything you want. Don't make your whole family and all your friends pay the hefty emotional price.

Doctors Rx Ask God to show you what you need to pursue, or release, in court.

When Winning Is Losing

If you want to discern whether or not to take someone to court or to put up a fight once you're there ask yourself, "I may have the *right*, but do I have the *responsibility*?"

Sarah Jane had legal grounds to file for more child support, but she had a good job, and her new husband was making enough to support them even if she didn't work. Sarah Jane had the right, but it was not necessarily the responsible thing to do. The kids were already well cared for. So what if her ex-husband should have been paying more? Was it Sarah's responsibility to discipline him? Or is it God's responsibility to work in the man's heart? It's not your responsibility to make your ex-spouse grow up, shape up, or pay up (if you don't need the money).

Frances, on the other hand, had a responsibility to her children to ask the courts to garnish her ex-husband's wages. She could barely make ends meet, and the kids needed expensive dental work. Her ex-husband could afford it.

Jesse had custody of his two boys most of the time and thought it unfair that his ex-wife was paying so little child support. After all, she'd remarried and didn't even have to work. But Jesse had to admit the kids did not need a thing.

What's been your experience in the court system? You may have the right, but is it right to be there?

Take Your Emotional X ray What's keeping me from dropping the unnecessary court battles, or from taking on an important fight for my children? What do I think Jesus would offer as wise counsel?

Take Custody of Your Heart

 If you do end up in court over your divorce, Scripture has some very practical advice:

- "Do not exploit the poor because they are poor and do not crush the needy in court, for the LORD will take up their case and will plunder those who plunder them" (Prov. 22:22, 23). It's pretty clear: No matter how expert your attorney may be, your greed and desire to get even won't reap for you more than you'll "pay" if the other side has the Lord as its attorney!
- "What you have seen with your eyes do not bring hastily to court, for what will you do in the end if your neighbor puts you to shame?" (Prov. 25:7, 8). In a rush to make your ex-spouse look bad, you may end up showing your own weaknesses. Judges or court-appointed psychiatrists may see you as the one who needs help.
- "If a wise man goes to court with a fool, the fool rages and scoffs, and there is no peace" (Prov. 29:9). Some people go round after round in court, staying stuck in pain and bitterness, and racking up thousands of dollars in legal fees. Sometimes it's better for you (your kids and your pocketbook, too) to bite the bullet if you know your ex-spouse is a "fool" who will not reasonably cooperate within the court system.

Don't forget the bigger courtroom where the Lord sits on the High Throne. He watches to see how much you trust him, love him, and are willing to let go of bitterness and fear.

Daily Dose of God's Word "The LORD takes his place in court; he rises to judge the people" (Isa. 3:13).

What You Can't Control

Don't Give Up, But Do Let Go

A scared child thrashing in the deep end of the pool reaches out to get control. His motive? Preserving his life.

A father in court who fights like a tiger so his ex-wife can't get the lion's share of their assets wants control. His motive? Preserving his financial security.

A mother in court who tries to get her husband's visitation reduced wants control. Her motive? Preserving her influence over her children or maneuvering for more child support.

All three want control. The child's reasons are valid. The adults' may or may not be. If the father has already given up more than half the estate, is paying above-average child support, and is being financially ruined by the divorce, we might understand his fight for control.

If the mother knows her husband will abuse the children as he did during their marriage, we understand her need for control.

But no matter how noble our motives, there are things in life we can *never* control. When that happens, we can choose to chase the desires, run ourselves ragged pursuing righteousness, or we can surrender to what is. We can accept the bad with the good and remind ourselves that a loving, merciful God is ready to throw us a lifeline when we feel like we're out of control.

Take Your Emotional Temperature What is keeping you from accepting the things you cannot control? Is it:

Fear of not getting the "I wants"?
Fear of injustice?
Lack of trust in God?

Too Much Is Too Much

Margie was livid that she couldn't control her ex-husband's time with the kids. "He indulges them, doesn't discipline them, and lets his girlfriend spend the night."

Steve was angry that his ex-wife bought the children expensive toys but wouldn't help them with their homework.

Vicki's ex never took the kids to church, and Frank's former spouse let the kids drink beer when they were only teenagers.

All of these divorced parents are focused on what they can't control and allowing the anger to rob them of precious energy, peace, and joy.

Control is not a bad word. We need control of the car we drive and the thoughts we think. Self-control is a virtue, one of the fruits of the Spirit. It's *excessive control* that keeps us in bondage. If you find yourself trying to control to excess, or in areas where God has not given you the responsibility for control, try these four steps to get back on track:

1. Identify all the areas that you can and can't control. Write them down.
2. Stop focusing on areas you can't control, then grieve the loss.
3. Start appreciating areas you can control.
4. Remind yourself about the bigger picture, and ask for God's help.

Take a Heart Pill Repeat daily: *Self-control* helps me avoid *excessive control.*

Megalomaniac Managers

Lenora tried to micromanage her son's time with his father on weekends. She hounded her ex-husband about the type of toothpaste their son should use, the food he ate, his precise bedtime, and what he should wear to church. Lenora could not let go. By refusing to accept what she couldn't control, she ended up locked in an exhausting dance of anger.

Except in cases where it's specifically spelled out by the court, this is a typical list of what you used to be able to control, but now, after divorce, can't control:

Anything that goes on in the other home.
Anything he or she says to the kids.
Anything he or she does with the kids.
Anything he or she gives the kids.
What he or she lets them wear.
What doctor or counselor he or she lets them see.
What church they attend or don't attend.
Where they sleep or what they eat.
What companions he or she lets them have.
How well he or she follows the visitation agreement.

As hard as it may be, you must accept the loss of control in these areas.

Talk to the Doctor *Lord, please help me move through the grief process and come to a place of acceptance where I trust that you are in control.*

What You Can Control

Bite Your Tongue!

You can control your tongue. It's tempting to gossip or bad-mouth people involved in your divorce: your ex-spouse, his family or friends, the attorney who snared you in court, or the adulterous lover who used to be your best friend. While part of recovery is "telling your story" you need to try to keep character assassination out of the pages.

God's Word warns us of the sins of the tongue: the *lying tongue* (Prov. 6:17), the *manipulative tongue* (Ps. 5:9), the *proud tongue* (Ps. 12:3, 4), the *swift tongue* (Prov. 18:13), the *slandering tongue* (Rom. 1:30), the *tale-bearing tongue* (Prov. 18:8), the *cursing tongue* (Rom. 3:13, 14), the *piercing tongue* (Prov. 12:18), and even the *silent tongue* (Eccles. 3:7).

Exactly how can you tame your tongue?

Well, I'm no cardiologist, but I believe there is a direct link metaphorically between the muscle we call the tongue and the muscle we call the heart. What's in the heart comes out on the tongue. If you still have bitterness, anger, or a wounded spirit from your divorce, it will be revealed in the way you speak to or about others, or in the seething quiet where you refuse to speak at all.

Controlling the tongue, therefore, starts with healing the heart. Genuine kindness in our hearts is a healing balm to others, poured out in our words of affirmation, support, truthfulness, and forgiveness.

Daily Dose of God's Word "Pleasant words are a honeycomb, sweet to the soul and healing to the bones" (Prov. 16:24).

It's Your Choice

My favorite coffee drink, especially after a long afternoon of shopping, is a latte. My choices are hot or iced, regular or decaf, venti or enorme, triple shot or quad, no topping or whipped cream, regular or nonfat milk. It's ridiculous, I know, but I love it all.

Once when I couldn't find a Starbucks at a mall, I immediately felt deprived when I realized I'd have to settle for generic coffee in one size. I had no choices! We often demand what we want, how we want it, and when we want it, don't we? Freedom of choice was what brought our forefathers to this land. The right to choose has been, and still is, at the heart of political furor. It's no wonder we fight to preserve our choices; next to life itself, the ability to think and choose is one of God's greatest gifts to us. But if what we choose—or want to choose—is not consistent with God's choice for us, we actually lose our freedom. Our heart gets clogged with desires and bound by anger, hurt, or resentment.

What's the antidote? Acknowledging who is in control, appreciating the choices we have, and remembering that being able to choose is a gift, not a right. I could focus on not being able to choose Starbucks, or I could be thankful for the seemingly small but incredible gift of being able to get a hot cup of coffee whenever I want one.

You can focus on your lack of choices after a divorce—what you can't control—or the many gifts, privileges, and graces that God grants you every day. It's your choice.

Daily Dose of God's Word "Do not be anxious about anything, but in everything, by prayer and petition, with thanksgiving, present your requests to God" (Phil. 4:6).

Mind Control

 You can't control other people, but you can control how you respond to them.

After my divorce I learned that the key to controlling my emotions was changing my thinking. The world reinforces selfish, obsessive thoughts of how to make the other pay, how to get what you deserve, why you should stay involved even when the person keeps hurting you, and even that you should hang in there so you can save or fix your ex-spouse. I replaced such thoughts with:

- *God loves that person as passionately and sweetly as he loves me. He has a special plan for him or her, and I need to get out of the way.*
- *God can do a much better job than I can on this person. Thankfully, I am not responsible for his or her growth, development, or salvation. I don't have to be a teacher or a rescuer.*
- *God did not put me in charge of making anyone pay. He wants me to forgive, to seek forgiveness, and to come to a place of genuine caring. But I don't have to get emotionally entangled with this person.*
- *God wants me to focus on **my** attitude, not the **other person's** actions.*

As I began to think these thoughts, my attitude and actions changed. Changing your thinking changes your heart. Renewing your thought patterns to conform to God's Word is a powerful weapon against pain. And it really puts you in control!

Daily Dose of God's Word "Do not conform any longer to the pattern of this world, but be transformed by the renewing of your mind" (Rom. 12:2).

Problem Solving

Filling Up Your Tool Kit

When I was young, Dad taught me how to string a bow and shoot an arrow into the hay target in our backyard. Mom taught me how to hold babies safely, warm their bottles, and pin their diapers without poking myself—or them! Celestine, our housekeeper, taught me how to make fresh peach cobbler with a flaky crust, and how to iron a man's shirt so there wasn't a wrinkle left. But no one taught me relationship problem-solving skills.

The older I get, the more I realize that most people have never been taught how to resolve conflicts. When there's a problem, we either ignore it and hope it will go away, avoid bringing it up but obsess over it, nag the other person to death without any resolution, or chase the other person down and cram it down their throat. None of these patterns solve problems.

Since we're called to love one another, we need to implement a way of thinking and acting that diffuses anger and solves problems. Our old ways of thinking and behaving may have contributed to our divorces and are probably keeping us engaged in ongoing struggles.

What keeps you from buying a book or taking a course on communication techniques or problem-solving skills? Too much work? Think you don't need it? I could never have made that peach cobbler without the cookbook and someone to mentor me.

Doctor's Rx Make a commitment to go to your favorite bookstore, or go on-line, and order a book about conflict resolution or communication techniques.

Getting Good Grades

In seventh grade I finally got a straight-A report card and I've been in love with A's ever since. Maybe that's why the items on my problem-solving checklist all start with A.

- Admit the Problem
  Admitting there's trouble brings you out of denial and into reality.

- Accept the Problem
  Imagine the worst that could happen; it helps you face fear and put trust back in God.

- Appreciate the Problem
  Every problem has the potential to become a pearl of great wisdom in your life. Look for the character quality you lack in the situation and that God might want to build in you.

- Attack the Problem
  You can always learn new ways to solve problems and communicate.

It was Alcoholics Anonymous, the worldwide support group also known as AA that popularized what I think is the perfect prayer for problem solving:

Talk to the Doctor *God, grant me the serenity to accept the things I cannot change, the courage to change the things I can, and the wisdom to know the difference.* (Serenity Prayer)

How Jesus Did It

When people came to Jesus with a problem, he used a four-step technique to help them that we can use today. It's not always easy, but if we keep it in mind, it will keep us on track:

Listen: Jesus didn't have an agenda. He listened to every word people said and was patient and thoughtful before he decided what to do or say. To listen well, we need to have a quiet spirit that trusts life's process and God's grace. Good listeners don't rush.

Lead: Jesus always made sure his response would help lead the person to the Father. Sometimes it was a direct leading, other times it was simply sharing a story or setting an example. Whether they're ready to be open to God or not, we're called to lead others by suggestion, example, or prayer to a place where they feel loved.

Love: Jesus could love even when he didn't trust. He knew the Pharisees were out to get him, but he willingly died for them, too. He showed love even when he didn't like what someone was doing by telling the person to go and sin no more. Jesus loved by wanting the very best for a person's soul, and by being willing to speak up, stay silent, or get out of the way if necessary.

Let Go: Jesus loved everyone, but he didn't hang on. He lovingly presented his message, shared his stories, and moved on. He never gave up faith, hope, or love for others, but he trusted the Father in all things. He knew how and when to let go.

Talk to the Doctor: *Lord, help me listen, lead, love, and let go as you did.*

Singleness

Wake Me When It's Over

Imagine being in the dark quiet of your room, all warm and cozy under your covers. In the middle of the night someone rushes in, flips on the bright light, rips off the bedspread, pulls you out of bed, and says, "Get dressed. We have to leave *now.*" Dazed, confused, and squinting as your eyes adjust to the light, you try to adjust yourself to this sudden change. Being single after divorce can be just as disorienting.

It doesn't matter whether you were relatively happy or miserable in your marriage when it ended; divorce takes you out of a comfort zone and throws you into an unknown world you have not visited for a long time. You can charge ahead into singleness in search of a quick replacement, stay in shock and pretend it hasn't happened, or hide in the dark hoping you'll never hurt again.

The season of singleness can seem to linger forever. Even if you feel blessed relief for a while, it's usually not long before you'll begin to feel lonely. *Will I find someone I can trust? Will he or she really love me? Where is he, when will I find her, and how will I know he or she's the one? If I marry again, will my new spouse be faithful? What if I never have love . . . or sex again?* The fear of the unknown can smother us with a blanket of anxiety and keep us tangled in the sheets of insecurity. We hate being in the dark.

God is still with you. He won't flip the switch so you can see the whole future, but he will shine his light on you one day at a time. You can rest in that assurance.

Daily Dose of God's Word "Your word is a lamp to my feet and a light for my path." (Ps. 119:105)

Faith for Friday Night

 The phone rings. You pick it up and hear God's voice on the other end.

"Hello, Beloved. Just wanted to let you know I'm sending someone special into your life, but I can't tell you exactly when. Be ready." Click! He hangs up. What would you do?

I'd spend the time getting ready. I'd consider that "someone special" must want someone special in return. In the same way I clean my house when I know company's coming, I'd break my bad habits, get smarter, become more loving, seek greater wisdom, and strip my emotional closets of any garbage that was still in there.

Just like the house-cleaning project, done with an ice-cold soda and the stereo cranked up, I'd make my personal upgrade fun while I was working at it. And just like I check the clock every once in awhile and look out the door to see if my company is driving up, I'd keep watch for God's special someone to enter my life. If my company has not arrived yet, I use the extra time finding and fixing any last details until the house is spotless, so I wouldn't allow myself to be idle while waiting for God's man to show up. There's *always* something to fix!

Even though you don't get a personal phone call from God, you might want to consider your single season as a time to become the best person God intended you to be, regardless of when or whether someone special shows up. The worst-case scenario? The one you expect never shows. But you can always invite God to dinner. He's the best company!

Today's Treatment Read the parable of the ten virgins in Matthew 25:1–13. You don't know "the day or the hour" . . . or even who . . . but you can have fun getting ready. Don't forget to sing while you sweep!

Busy As a Beaver?

 Did you know beavers can hold their breath for forty-five minutes?

Just the thought of holding my breath that long makes me feel lightheaded. I suppose God designed the beaver to hold his breath so long because he needed to be under water to build his home.

Being single after divorce is a time when we try to rebuild our homes, and we may find ourselves holding our breath for many reasons: waiting for the money to come, waiting for the pain to go away, or waiting for someone new to come along. Maybe we feel like we're drowning in loneliness. Maybe we've already built a dam to keep everyone out so we feel safe from a flood of emotions. No matter our response, we can get exhausted from the emotional energy it takes to protect ourselves.

Prayerfully consider any heavy logs you might be carrying through the deep part of the creek. What responsibilities do you need to hold on to, and which ones can you release? Jesus invites exhausted singles, "Come to me, all you who are weary and burdened, and I will give you rest" (Matt. 11:28). If you let God work in you and with you to rebuild your lives as singles, you'll never have to work alone.

And you won't have to hold your breath.

Take Your Emotional X ray What fears are keeping you from breathing deeply? Are you waiting to exhale?

Dog Days

If I read one more singles' advice column that says buy a pet or sign up for volunteer work, I'll scream. Not that those aren't good ideas for some people, but they don't address the real issues, and they don't help people who are allergic to cats or hate poodles.

Here are some other things to consider when you're single:

- Remember that this time in your life is for a season, not for eternity.
- Remember no one is ever perfectly content. God saves that for heaven!
- If you're really brave, call up your ex-spouse and ask him what character flaws he thinks you should work on.
- Don't limit yourself to just one kind of growth or change. Make a list of what you can do to develop whole beauty— physically, mentally, emotionally, and spiritually.
- Recall a passion you've had but put on the shelf for a while. Take it down, dust it off, and go for it!
- Remember you're still healing. Take it easy and get lots of rest. Give yourself permission to spoil yourself silly once in a while.
- Trust God whenever you feel bad about being single. He has a plan for you.
- Thank God every day for the gift of singleness, because through it he can give you pearls of not only great wisdom but peace.

Doctor's Rx Tell yourself this whenever you need to hear it: Just because I'm single doesn't mean I have to let myself go to the dogs!

Waiting

Running Down the Aisle

My friend Shana Graham, a blue-eyed beauty, wife, and mother of four, won the title Mrs. California two years in a row. She told me about her early dating experiences and her romance with her husband, Robert. At nineteen, the two of them fell madly in love and rushed into marriage after only three months of dating. Once married, the couple had terrible marriage problems that lasted over ten years. They fought, separated, reconciled, fought again, drained their finances, and exhausted their families. "It was a living hell on earth," Shana reflected. She told me it was only with mutual commitment to their vows, God's grace, hard work, thousands of hours of counseling, help from friends, prayers, and nights of endless tears, that they made it through the tough times. I asked Shana what she regretted most.

"That's easy. Not waiting."

Shana admitted that life would have been much different if she and Robert had set a date to marry and then given themselves time to wait. "I realize I made my decisions on my emotions, and by not waiting a longer time to test the relationship, I only invited trouble," Shana said.

After divorce, waiting for romance can keep us on edge or set us up to rush into another set of problems. There are usually two reasons we can't wait: we want it *now* or we don't trust God will give us what we need in his time. By not waiting, we usually only invite trouble.

Talk to the Doctor *Father, I have trouble sometimes trusting you. Please help me relax and wait for whatever "title" you have for me in the future.*

Slow Cooking on Low Heat

 Why do we hate to wait after divorce? Why do we rush back into relationships?

We hate to wait because we're emotionally starved. Have you ever gone grocery shopping when you're starving? Relationships can affect us the same way. When we're not getting enough healthy companionship, love, emotional support, friendship, encouragement, and social activity, we're more likely to jump into a relationship we're not ready for, one that is not healthy, or we start devouring what does not yet belong to us.

We hate to wait because we have little else that really satisfies us. If we rush into relationships and fail to give them time to develop, then we probably haven't cultivated a wide variety of other satisfying interests. We might be busy at work or parenting, but are we doing something else that we absolutely love and that feeds our souls? If not, why not?

We hate to wait because we think love will never come again. Little children think Christmas will never come. Maybe it's that childish attitude that keeps us impatient.

We hate to wait because we have microwave mentality. We want to find someone potentially yummy, quickly scan their ingredients, pop them in the oven, and get married. We get everything else we want in a hurry . . . why not new love, too?

Take Your Emotional Temperature I get so anxious sometimes that I actually get heated up. What's stopping me from cooling it?

A Surprise Worth Waiting For

What's so good about waiting?

Waiting develops patience. Patience is a virtue that you can, and should, use many times over in all your relationships. If you want people to be patient with you, you need to develop patience for others.

Waiting gives you more time to work on yourself. Remember the more mature, well-balanced, and emotionally healthy you become, the higher caliber spouse you'll attract.

Waiting allows time to reveal truth. In the sixties when I was a Girl Scout, I sold flower seeds door-to-door to raise money for summer camp. I planted some marigold seeds, having no idea if the flowers would be red, gold, or yellow. Only time would tell. Waiting helps you see someone's true colors.

Waiting can reap unexpected rewards. I learned lots of lessons about waiting when I was little. As the oldest of nine children, I was expected to wait until all the younger kids had their turn or made their choice. When I did, Mom and Dad would often give me something extra for waiting. Waiting can be its own reward.

Maybe you are not waiting for a new relationship, but you *do* seem to be waiting for *something* . . . something you can't pinpoint.

Take Your Emotional X ray What are you waiting for that's keeping you from being content? Ask God to show you.

Grace

Life Is Full of Party Favors

Grace is sweet blessings and bounty heaped upon us for no reason other than we are deeply loved. We don't earn grace or deserve it. Grace is a gift. Grace can be finding favor despite our unfavorable standing. We know we'll get that from God, but what about from others?

After my divorce, my social life unraveled. I lost fun friends whom I'd met through my husband. I obviously was not invited to any more of his family gatherings since that would make others uncomfortable. Church members began to shun me. The women who used to greet my husband and me on Sunday mornings now looked away awkwardly when I entered alone. My invitation to the Christmas party for church volunteers was somehow overlooked, and I wasn't invited to the same social gatherings. Some of my friends quit asking me to dinner parties because now that I was single I didn't fit. It was a hurtful time.

Divorce can make us realize how desperately we need grace, especially when we "fall out of favor" with the family, our social circles, and even the church. Thankfully, God, who loves us so much, is pleased to send his grace to us through other people. For me it was my former mother-in-law. Despite the painful breakup and the fact I was no longer part of her family, it was Marion who reached out to me in love by inviting me to lunch, keeping in touch through phone calls, and for years afterward remembering to send me birthday and Christmas cards. It was nothing more than grace. Amazing, isn't it?

Doctor's Rx Stop and look carefully at the people and circumstances in your life that, despite the pain of divorce, have been blessings to you. They are there. They are grace.

A Precious Pedicure

Jesus got up from the table, untied his sash, and removed his outer robe. Then he took a long towel, wrapped it around his waist, and tied a knot. The disciples watched in silence, wondering what their Master was going to do.

Jesus then filled a basin with fresh water and approached Peter. Kneeling down, the Master began to wash Peter's feet. Peter was shaken. He felt unworthy of receiving such special, humbling treatment from the one he believed was the Messiah. And he *was* unworthy.

The Lord knew that his friends were weak and sinful. He knew that within hours Peter, who professed to love him so deeply, would deny him. Peter did not deserve, or earn, the physical cleansing that represented the spiritual cleansing that was coming. But that's precisely what grace is: an undeserved, unearned favor in God's eyes. Jesus told his disciples he was setting them an example—that they should give such unmerited love and service to others.

As difficult as it may seem, you and I are called after divorce to be grace-full with those who do not deserve it. We are to be generous with our kindness despite the hurt, pain, and suffering we may have experienced in the past or will experience in the future.

Who has betrayed you in your divorce? Who has denied you because of their own fear or self-protectiveness? Has God put you in a position where you can bestow grace?

Daily Dose of God's Word "I have set you an example that you should do as I have done for you." (John 13:15)

Give It Away . . . for Free

Laurie did not deserve any favors. An angry, controlling divorcee, she constantly fought her ex-husband, Tom, over custody and visitation issues regarding their six-year-old son. Tom, who was remarried, longed to have more time with his son, but Laurie always refused. On special occasions such as his relative's weddings, family reunions, or holiday gatherings, Tom would beg Laurie for a few extra hours so their son could participate.

One night, when the boy and his father were returning to Laurie's home after the weekend, they called her to ask for an extra fifteen minutes to stop and get an ice cream. For years Laurie had kept records of anytime her ex-husband was five minutes late dropping their son off and had filed repeated frivolous complaints with the courts. As a result, he was careful to get her permission even for this short stop. Her son even got on the phone and asked too. "No," said Laurie. "It's important that your father stick to his agreement, honey. You need to come home now, and when you get here, I'll take you out for ice cream."

It was different when she wanted something, though. One day Laurie asked her ex-husband to forfeit his plans to chaperone their son and his friends on a weekend, school field trip so she could go instead. Some of the mothers were going, and she didn't want to be excluded. After years of selfishness, did she deserve, or had she earned, the favor? Definitely not. Even though he hated to do it, he knew what he should give her—grace—and he said yes.

Take Your Emotional X ray Is there anything blocking your heart from granting grace to your ex-spouse?

What's So Good about Divorce?

I have a secret. Some people won't understand, but maybe you will; when hurting people come to my divorce recovery seminars, they don't know it, and I don't tell them, but *in a way* I am glad they suffered the emotional heart attack of divorce. Let me explain.

When Lazarus was dying, his sisters, Martha and Mary, were deeply mournful. Their grief caused them to call out for Jesus. Their fear of Lazarus's impending death moved them to seek Jesus' help. In our lives, divorce can be like Lazarus's death. As painful as it is, it can be the event that causes us to call out to Jesus when maybe before the divorce we never called to him. Our fears and anxieties about money, loneliness, anger, or depression may move us to seek God's help more than we ever have before.

Lazarus, once dead, was brought back to life, but not because he'd earned it or deserved it. When Jesus restored life to Lazarus, it was grace freely given.

Do you recall what Jesus said when the messengers reported that his friend Lazarus had died? He didn't say, "Oh, I'm so sorry!" and he didn't seem sad at all. Instead, he said that he was *glad*! Jesus knew that death . . . like divorce . . . is not the end. He knew that if we let him, God can use bad things to reveal his glory and help us believe. Can you try to come to a place of thanksgiving for *your* divorce? Has it brought you closer to him? If so, rejoice.

Daily Dose of God's Word "So then he told them plainly, 'Lazarus is dead, and for your sake I am glad I was not there, so that you may believe.'" (John 11:14, 15)

Dating and Sex

Is It Time?

 How do you know when you're ready to date again? Take your emotional temperature with this checklist:

- *Dating brings up old memories:* Have you substantially healed from the hurt, anger, fear, or bitterness from your old relationship? How often do you still think of your ex? Milk cartons have expiration dates, but memories don't. Don't sour a new relationship with old bitterness. Remember: A whole woman attracts a whole man and vice versa. A wounded woman attracts a wounded man.
- *Dating brings up old emotions:* Do you still feel unsure of who you are, what you want in life, or where you're going? Do you mistrust the opposite sex or have an addictive need to be in a relationship? Dating is distracting. Unhealed emotions only hurt new relationships.
- *Dating the same old way will get you the same old trouble:* Can you take it slow, establish a trusting friendship first, and save sex for marriage? Becoming physically intimate too soon *blinds us* to our partner's character defects and *binds us* as "one flesh" so that it's almost impossible to get out of a bad relationship.

Doctor's Rx Resuming dating too quickly is like anesthesia for the heart. It helps to numb the pain of divorce, but we don't want to be asleep when we consider new relationships. Don't repeat old patterns with new people.

Great S.E.X.!

Do you remember married sex? After a fight everything seemed to be resolved when you fell into bed with each other and made love. The walls came down and it was exciting, calming, sweet, passionate, and at least for awhile, a promise of peace. When we're single after divorce, however, we need to keep up the walls to protect ourselves. For "safe" sex, try this definition:

S is for *surrender*. God designed your mind, heart, and body to work like a symphony together in sex. Surrendering your desires and your will to God's way and time can bring the Berlin Philharmonic into your life. Do it *your* way and you'll end up with "Row, Row, Row, Your Boat" and a heart that will eventually sink.

E is for *educate*. Even older singles who have been married can remain naively ignorant about sex. Use this time to educate yourself about how men and women were uniquely designed to respond to sex not just physically, but mentally, emotionally, and spiritually. Research. Read. Get ready.

X is for *cross out*. The media has sold us a worthless bill of goods about sex. There are more broken relationships than ever. Free sex is not free; it eventually demands a devastating price. Cross out what the world says. No more lurid romance novels or soft-porn magazines, movies, and videos. Replace media muck with intelligent, pure, enriching entertainment.

Daily Dose of God's Word "Like a city whose walls are broken down is a man who lacks self-control." (Prov. 25:28)

Take a Good Look

Benjamin Franklin said we should enter marriage with our eyes wide open and afterward keep our eyes half shut. That's especially good advice for divorced singles. Maybe you have already started dating. Maybe you rushed in and had your heart broken again and are now taking some time off from the opposite sex. Perhaps you're not even thinking about dating, waiting instead until the kids are grown. No matter where you are, your eyes should be open. Why? Because as exciting or as scary as it can be to think about, God might be bringing someone into your life when you least expect it. Keeping your eyes wide open will help you be ready. Here are some things to remember:

- Tolerating human weakness is strength inside marriage, but looking at someone through romantic eyes before we get to really know them can be the key to another failure. Get real this time. Trust God to open your eyes.
- Taking the time to take a good, hard look at another person is not being overly cautious or paranoid. Don't let anyone shame you for taking your time and being careful.
- Talking early on in the relationship about everything that is important to you is vital. Scrutinize and analyze this person with whom you plan to entrust your heart. Having faith in the future is different from foolish optimism.

Doctor's Rx Smart dating calls for magnifying glasses, not rose-colored glasses. Look hard in the present so your life will be rosier in the future.

Dream Dates

 My niece, Alethea, a single in her mid-twenties, shared a dream with me:

"I was walking along eating an ice-cream cone. Ice cream is *my favorite* treat!" she said with a huge grin on her dimpled face, then continued. "It was so good and I was so-o-o happy. All of a sudden the ice-cream scoop fell out of the cone and onto the ground into a pile of dirt, rocks, and fresh manure. I stood there looking at the ice cream and thinking, *Oh no!* I hated to admit I still wanted it. It wasn't totally covered and maybe . . . but then I thought, *No, Alethea, that's disgusting!* and tried to walk away. But I couldn't. I wanted it. Rose, I stood there fighting with myself to pick it up and eat it or walk away."

"E-w-w-w! Alethea, that *is* disgusting! What did you do?"

Alethea looked at me with horror and admitted, "I ATE IT!" We screamed in unison and both dissolved into laughter. I told my niece I thought it was a very clear dream. She'd been dating a young man who was smart, handsome, and charming, and who adored her. But he was also pressuring her to have sex, warning her at the same time that he was not ready for marriage. Alethea admitted she loved the flattery and attention of the relationship; in fact she was starving for it, but she knew it would make her sick if she stayed in it. I understood my niece, because in the past I, too, had tried to make relationships that were not good for me work out somehow.

Take Your Emotional X ray A gracious God will speak to you through your dreams if you won't listen to him when you're awake. What is God trying to tell you about relationships in your life, and what's keeping you from hearing him?

Spoiling Your Appetite

I remember being in fifth grade and waiting for my mother to bring my lunch to school. I was starving! Usually I tried to have a bowl of Rice Krispies in the morning, but with getting bathed, dressed, and trying to help some of my eight younger siblings get ready, I didn't always have time to eat. That morning we were out of lunchmeat and the Wonder Bread was moldy, so Mom promised she'd go to the store and bring me my lunch. Unfortunately, my mom was never on time for anything, so I sat in the cafeteria as others opened their lunch boxes and ate. The smells of peanut butter and chocolate milk drove me nuts!

Finally I couldn't stand it any more. A girl next to me offered the crust from her sandwich, and I took it. Yuck! It had Miracle Whip on it, not mayonnaise. The teacher made others share with me also, but I got leftovers like a bruised banana no one wanted. I hated it, but I ate every bit because I was so hungry. Wouldn't you know, Mom finally showed up with a yummy lunch after I had eaten the scraps. But by then I was too full.

When we're starving, we'll eat anything, even if it isn't good. Maybe it's because we haven't taken responsibility for keeping our lives full of other good things, and we end up always needy. Maybe it's because we want God to bring us someone "on time," and we just can't wait. When he shows up with the honey, we're too full to eat. Are you keeping yourself full of other interests, pleasures, and delights so you won't be starving for just *any* relationship?

Daily Dose of God's Word "He who is full loathes honey, but to the hungry even what is bitter tastes sweet." (Prov. 27:7)

Remarriage

School Days

Do you recall childhood summers? You just couldn't *wait* to get out of school. You probably spent weeks taking trips, having sleepovers with your friends, having fun, and maybe even building some new type of playhouse in the backyard. But then came the doldrums. The weather got hotter in August, and your allowance was gone, spent on too many souvenirs at the beach. You grew tired of the same trips to the park, the same slumber parties, and the same games. You wanted something new. Maybe you surprised yourself by even starting to look forward to going back to school.

The summer of singleness after divorce can be relief from a troubled marriage. You might feel a sense of freedom and get back to playing and planning fun things in your life. But after awhile, you can get bored or restless and long for someone to love again. You might begin to long to return to marriage.

Remarriage is a mixed bag, just like school was for us as kids. Many things will be new, and hopefully we'll have become smarter as we advance into a new marriage. There will again be the same homework, tests, and times we have to stay late. Every marriage has ups and downs, and sometimes in a second marriage, we may long for the sweet days of our single summer. If God opens the door of remarriage for you, just make sure you still don't have childish fantasies about it.

Daily Dose of God's Word "When I was a child, I talked like a child, I thought like a child, I reasoned like a child. When I became a man, I put childish ways behind me." (1 Cor. 13:11)

Listen to the Man!

After divorce, we can become supersensitive to the criticism of others. We can doubt our decisions and be fearful of making more mistakes. With a bellyful of rejection from divorce, we don't want to pile more on our plate. Sometimes we do what others suggest instead of using our own heads, following our own hearts, and obeying God's will for us.

If you consider, talk about, or plan on getting married again, be prepared. It's something that will generate strong opinions among your friends, family, and pastor.

While Jesus hung on the cross, minutes away from gaining salvation for us, the bad thief hung inches away but miles apart in his own opinions about the crucifixion. This fearful but arrogant man didn't accept what Jesus was doing; in fact he challenged Jesus to use his powers to come down off the cross. But Jesus had used his head, his heart, and all of his resources to discern his Father's will for him and had chosen to carry it out—regardless of how desperate or foolish it looked to others.

If you're considering remarriage, make your decision based on what you know of God's will for you. Use your head by reading, seeking wise counsel from godly mentors, and praying.

Remarriage could be heaven or hell, but let God's Spirit lead your heart. Don't let anyone else's opinion steal your power or rob you of joy.

Daily Dose of God's Word "Then he said, 'Jesus, remember me when you come into your kingdom.'" (Luke 23:42)

Happy Trails to You

I sat inches away from the black-and-white television, my ten-year-old legs crossed Indian style, neck craned, arms crossed, and eyes glued intently on Doris Day as Calamity Jane. I wanted to be a scout like her. Scouts bravely galloped ahead of the wagon train and searched for safe paths through unknown territory. They went thirsty for days, but made maps of where the water was when they found it. Grizzly bears, savage arrows, and dead-ends were some of the dangers that sent scouts back to camp wounded or scarred. At night they'd lie on their bedrolls, looking up at the stars and feeling lonely, but knowing they were providing a service that would save lives.

A service that would save lives. Now that's something divorced people can do when they enter a second marriage. If you've been divorced, others might see you, or you might see yourself, like those scouts—bruised, battered, and scarred for life. After my divorce, I felt pretty beat up. Scouts wore their scars proudly, as signs that they knew what was ahead and had survived the worst. If our scars are healed, they can help instill confidence in others who need to trust someone who's "been there." In fact, the more weathered the scout, the more revered he or she was for knowing the trails and dangers ahead.

A new spouse and family can benefit from your previous experience. You can ride shotgun and keep an eye out for danger in others' relationships and in your own. You'll know the paths to avoid this time and be able to help guide your partner in the right direction. There's no need for feeling shame.

Today's Treatment Don't be afraid to saddle up. Learn to honor the fact that despite your scars you have incredibly valuable wisdom and experience to share.

New Life

Out of the Dark

The doctors told me I was born with a small hole in my heart, but it's nothing like the hole Linda Jacobs described to me. Linda shared how God has worked on her heart through a powerful mental picture.

"I see a huge hole in my heart. It's a gigantic cavern that I keep trying to fill. I throw my close friend into the cavern, but he just becomes a tiny speck in the dark. I take all the videos that play in my mind and throw them in, hoping to fill the void, but they aren't enough. Everything I can lay my hands on—job, kids, friends—I throw into the heart hole, but the cavern is so large and so deep that all I see are little specks floating around.

"Suddenly I'm aware of standing on the side of the pit and sensing God in the distance, watching me and waiting. I feel a calmness begin to flood over me, and in an instant I know that he can completely fill the cavern. I let him. Peace, happiness, joy, and laughter begin to fill up the hole in my heart and I feel serene. I remember that his true love is what my heart needs in order to heal."

In the Old Testament, God's people had heavy hearts. Because they had been unfaithful to him, it seemed like a huge cavern separated them from his love. But God was . . . and ever is . . . merciful. God told them not to focus on the past, but to be encouraged by the new life he would bring into their relationships. He wants to give you the same new life.

Daily Dose of God's Word "Forget the former things; do not dwell on the past. See, I am doing a new thing! Now it springs up; do you not perceive it?" (Isa. 43:18, 19)

Rising to the Occasion

Have you ever had a paper cut? It's amazing something so harmless can slice right through your skin and cause it to hurt for the rest of the day. How about a little hangnail? Just a tiny tear in the skin around your cuticle can cause intense pain. Scraped knees are killers too. Just the other day my niece Hayley fell off her bike, ran into the house, and screamed at the top of her lungs, "AUNT R-O-S-I-E!" I thought a car had hit her the way she wailed over an inch of delicate skin that had been scraped and was only slightly bleeding.

Now . . . imagine a crown of thorns pressed into your flesh.

Jesus endured the whip lashes on his body and nails in his hands and feet. The lance in his side pierced close to his heart. All the heartbreak of divorce and the pain we feel in our hearts can't compare to the agonizing pain our Lord suffered for us. After his death, he was laid in a tomb, a dark, deep cavern in a hillside like the cavern that can be in our hearts after divorce. Christ knows the pain you've felt and may still feel, and he knows the dark, deep places into which we sometimes sink.

But the story didn't end for Jesus there, and it's not over for you. After the suffering, after the dark cave, came new life for Jesus. And new life awaits you, too. That is his promise. Alleluia, alleluia!

Daily Dose of God's Word "The angel said to the women, 'Do not be afraid, for I know that you are looking for Jesus, who was crucified. He is not here; he has risen, just as he said. Come and see the place where he lay.'" (Matt. 28:5, 6)

Your Own Resurrection

 Easter morning comes every year with joyful songs and fragrant lilies.

Our Lord died for us and rose from the dead only once, and once was enough. But his death and resurrection are eternal and ongoing in that for every generation that is born, his sacrifice is applied again for each person. Jesus' death and resurrection are ongoing in that with every death we feel after divorce—the death of our family, our hopes, our dreams—we have the promise of continued resurrection in our hearts through him.

The resurrection story is all about the same things you've experienced through divorce: love that's been spurned, trust that's been violated, and faith that's been shaken. The Master Physician invites you to come out of the tomb where he will heal your heart.

He calls you to love again after your love has been rejected.

He calls you to trust again after trust has been betrayed.

He calls you to believe again after your faith has been shaken.

He who heals hearts has a heart full of love for you. He who *is* life will give new life to you. He wants to make miracles happen in your life, starting today.

Doctor's Rx Spend some quiet time alone today with God, even if it's only for a few minutes, away from the office, out of the house, where no one can distract you. Sit still, quiet your thoughts, and just listen.

Your One True Love

Homemade Love

Do you remember the story of the Gingerbread Man? The baker carefully sifted the flour, grated the spices, and stirred the butter to create a sugary masterpiece. After the Gingerbread Man was finished baking, he tore himself off the cookie sheet and ran out the front door of the baker's house shouting, "Run, run, run, just as fast as you can! You can't catch me, I'm the Gingerbread Man!"

Out into the world the disobedient little delicacy ran. On the way he met many strange animals, most of which wanted to eat him. He had a few close calls, but he was determined and clever enough to evade them, laughing and chanting to each as he ran away, "You can't catch me, I'm the Gingerbread Man!"

Do you recall the tragic end of the story? A wily fox tricked the little bakery goody into getting onto his back, and as they crossed a deep stream, the Gingerbread Man had to climb up closer to the fox's head. Too late! The fox flicked his head back, opened his mouth, and gobbled the cookie up. God is like the baker, and we are his sweet creation. He made us for his pleasure and enjoyment, but we have run away from him to pursue our own wills, not his.

Although he has given us other people to love and love us in return, they are only part of his plan to get us to come home. Our Maker can even use tough times—like divorce—to bring us back home. We were not created for others; we were created for him, our One True Love.

Daily Dose of God's Word "Come, let us bow down in worship, let us kneel before the LORD our Maker." (Ps. 95:6)

Let Him Entertain You!

Bob Hope turned one hundred years old in May 2003. The singing, dancing comedian first shuffled onto the vaudeville stage in 1924 and later went into radio, stage, movies, and television. Hope's daughter, Linda, recalls a sweet memory of him: Often when she and her brother ate breakfast and got ready for school, their father would do a silly soft-shoe routine and shuffle out the door and off to Paramount Studios.

Perhaps Bob's greatest public contribution was his enduring sacrifice to bring laughter and entertainment to over ten million American troops in peacetime and during four wars—WWII, the Korean War, Vietnam, and the Persian Gulf War. His act always included a full stage production of songs, dance, music, and humor, and no expense was spared to bring our men and women in distant lands the light and laughter they needed. Many a young soldier, some soon marching off to their deaths, had their last lighthearted moments thanks to Bob Hope.

Once a corporal and his men walked miles for Hope's famous show but missed it. Bob Hope found out, packed up the entire troupe, caught up with the stranded soldiers, and did his complete act just for the small band of men in the middle of nowhere.

God will do that for you. Divorce can leave you feeling lost, stranded, and like you've missed the great show. But he will track you down wherever you are and bring the "show" to you. He loves you that much.

Daily Dose of God's Word "I love those who love me, and those who seek me find me." (Prov. 8:17)

A Passionate Pursuit

The Old Testament is a centuries-old love story of a passionate God who pursued his beloved people. The New Testament is the story of a still-loving God who made good on his promises and redeemed his unfaithful beloved by sacrificing himself for her.

Every one of us—man, woman, or child—wants someone who loves us so much that he would die for us. Well we already have him, and he already did.

After my failed marriage I fell to my knees in sorrow and repentance for having always pursued marriage and parenting as the ultimate happiness and fulfillment. Marriage and family are not bad desires; they are good things created to give us pleasure and to model God's love for us. But when we desire them more than we desire to know, love, and serve God, they become distractions . . . or maybe even fatal attractions!

When I began to release my grip on my dreams, God made real dreams come true. The casual dating relationship I'd had with him flamed into fiery passion for his Word, his presence, and his Spirit.

God is always calling to you, wooing you to him. Your courtship with him will not be without its ups and downs. You and I may be fickle, but he is faithful. His desire is for you . . . all of you.

Daily Dose of God's Word "I belong to my lover, and his desire is for me." (Song of Songs 7:10)

Seeking a Soul Mate

 A man wants a wife who will:
Always support and encourage him
Give him the freedom to make mistakes without holding
them against him
Open herself to receive him
Give of herself to him
Love him unconditionally

A woman wants a husband who will:
Pursue her, provide for her, and protect her
Cherish and treasure her
Be faithful and loyal
Bring her gifts of his love
Take her and ravish her with ecstasy

We are deeply blessed when we find such a spouse, but he or she will never be perfect. Have you thought that God, your One True Love, possesses every one of these things and more? Have you been looking in the wrong place to find healing for your broken heart?

Talk to the Doctor *Lord, help me to look past the love I seek on earth, so that I may pursue you and receive you at once.*

Happily Ever After

God is all that is sweet and tender in feminine strength. He is all that is strong and powerful in masculine might.

He is all that is good about Father, Mother, and Friend. He's vibrant, powerful, and perfect. He gave you life and calls you by name. He knows every inch of you, inside and out and adores you despite your flaws. He sees in you what no one else sees, and he values you more than life itself.

He sends you flowers in the springtime and baskets of fruit in the summer. He brings you sunshine in the mornings and rainbows to let you know he is still with you even in the tough times.

He would never leave you in a rut, so he sends the change of seasons to spice up your life. When it's hot, he sends shade and cool water. When it's cold, he provides you with the heat of a fire and the comfort of warm wool.

He promises to meet your needs, dry your tears, and be your strength in time of trouble. He is the Rock on which you can build your life, your home, and your family. He will be your faithful spouse. He will be father to your children and love them more than you ever could.

He is the maker of heaven and earth. He is power and glory and might, and at his name every knee shall bow and every tongue shall confess him as Lord.

He will never betray you or abandon you, and he will heal your broken heart.

He loves you. He is with you always . . . even after divorce, even until the end of time.

Daily Dose of God's Word "I have summoned you by name; you are mine." (Isa. 43:1)

Rose Sweet is a sparkling communicator. She is available to church and civic groups as a speaker, lecturer, and seminar leader—on a wide variety of inspirational and motivational topics. Rose can be contacted at:

Rose Sweet
73-241 Hwy 111 #3D
Palm Desert, CA 92260
(760) 346-9401
Email: RoseSweet523@aol.com
Web page: www.RoseSweet.com